Advance Praise for
Lay an Egg and Make Chicken Soup

"Thoughtful. Clear. Concise. Based on his personal experience, Arie Brish creates an easy-to-use new cartography on how innovation should be viewed in all organizations, regardless of the industry. He tackles the fundamentals of innovation and breaks it down so the reader can understand the concept; its key issues, interrelationships, and interdependencies; and its impact on business—[all] illustrated through many examples and key takeaways in each chapter. If you are a leader or want to be one, this is an important read, regardless of the stage of your business. If you want to deliver lasting results in an organization, get and read this relevant book."

—Dr. Elizabeth Danon-Leva, Change Management Strategies, Culture & Communications Consultant, U.S.

"The title and the content are so interesting! Full of insights. I like the book."

—Eng. Alex Dumas, CEO, L.I.G Energy, and former Member of Parliament, Rwanda

"A shrewd perspective on why some products thrive and others inevitably never leave the egg. Great examples that illustrate how some companies were able to thrive while others inevitably [became] obsolete. One of the lines that meant a lot to me was 'Don't try to be better; be different.' That basically summed up the core value of any amazing product."

—Colin Duffy, high school student, and founder & CEO of Coral View, U.S.

"Great work and approach for innovators as product managers, executives, or entrepreneurs. The flow makes sense and the wrap-up section gives a diverse set of insights that need to be considered. Innovative leaders hear many opinions on how to proceed yet insights are rare. *Lay an Egg and Make Chicken Soup* is a diamond mine of insights for successful innovation."

—Michael Heflin, COO, Sprout Tiny Homes, U.S.

"Comprehensive and enjoyable view of the whole innovation process, with a huge number of real-life examples. Very good, reads well."

—Bill Matthews, Chairman, BBC Pension Trust Limited, U.K.

"Short and concise, very easy to read. It is almost like a textbook; [the] linking between chapters is a nice touch. Actual business cases from many different industries [are] very useful."

—Bunsaku Nagai, Country Manager, Technoprobe, Japan

"I really enjoyed reading the book. It was fun, and that says everything. It was as if we were sitting together and discussing it. The direct, easy style is captivating and makes the reader want to continue going forward."

—Dr. Gershon Yaniv, CEO, DisperSol Technologies, LLC, U.S.

ARIE BRISH

LAY AN EGG

AND MAKE

CHICKEN SOUP

The Holistic Innovation Process
from Concept to Market Expansion

This book is dedicated to the hundreds of supervisors, mentors, colleagues, subordinates, mentees, and clients from whom I've learned so much about innovation in business. This book is the collective wisdom and lessons learned from all of them.

"All the great ideas and visions in the world are worthless if they can't be implemented rapidly and efficiently."

—Colin L. Powell, former U.S. Secretary of State

"Productivity and efficiency can be achieved only step by step with sustained hard work, relentless attention to details, and insistence on the highest standards of quality and performance."

—J. R. D. Tata, founder of the Tata Group

CONTENTS

INNOVATION, NEW PRODUCTS, AND SUCCESS

Innovation is the lifeblood of any business. Any business must innovate continuously if it doesn't want to become a follower.

Toyota realized the value of innovation and created a system of innovation that produces one million new ideas per year! That is two new ideas per minute. (Matthew E. May's *In Pursuit of Elegance: Why the Best Ideas Have Something Missing* offers insights into that system based on his having been a close adviser to Toyota for nearly a decade.) The innovation process, from idea conception to market expansion, is a multidisciplinary holistic one. Most executives are familiar with a few of the aspects, which they were exposed to during their earlier career, but very few C-suite leaders have hands-on experience with all the disciplines.

That reality became my motivation for writing this book. The main purpose of *Lay an Egg and Make Chicken Soup* is to introduce the multifaceted new products or services process to those executives who need a broader look at business innovation and how all the moving parts are supposed to work together. The people that will benefit the most from this book are founders of start-ups, CEOs, general managers, CFOs, venture capitalists, corporate directors, product managers, and new business owners.

This book will also be valuable to any executive who deals with new products, even if his or her focus is only on one aspect of the process, because you will become a better team player by familiarizing yourself with your colleagues' responsibilities and challenges.

A successful new product has multiple ingredients that must be mixed together strategically. Leaving out any one ingredient may spoil the whole dish. Those ingredients include sparking a vision, getting it funded, having it designed, managing the operation, developing the synergistic ecosystem, marketing it, selling it, and supporting the customers to keep them happy so they will spread the word among their friends and colleagues. Start all over ASAP, of course, to keep the competition from catching up with you.

This book provides you with a glimpse of all the disciplines involved in the new products process. Although I've concentrated on devoting one chapter per topic, these disciplines are interrelated. So you'll see some repetition of ideas and nuances: for example, a discussion of e-commerce in chapter 7 in the context of business models and again in chapter 13 in the context of sales channels. I intentionally analyze the same topic (financial planning, risks) from different angles as well as show the links between different departments and disciplinary perspectives.

I have been blessed to work in multiple industries. One

important lesson I learned by doing so is that there is a great deal of experience one industry can learn from another. "Business as usual" in one industry might be a radical, out-of-the-box concept in another. In *Lay an Egg and Make Chicken Soup*, I have tried to cover many industries to expose the reader to different ways of doing things in different vertical segments. Some of the verticals covered in this book are technology, automotive, cyber security, communication, mobile phones, chemicals, fashion, entertainment, gaming, construction, transportation, food, sex, jewelry, health, energy, sports, alcohol, gangs, banking, insurance, airlines, aircraft, religion, tattoos, and—last but not least—poultry farming. Some more, some less.

The case studies are likewise geographically diverse, and in some examples, I underscore the difference between corporate innovation and innovation at a start-up. When the differences between the two are significant, I address both separately.

Many of the case studies are intentionally old. But I've included a few modern case studies too, of course, to strike a balance between the remote past and the most recent past (i.e., the present). My motivation for illustrating my points with the old examples is twofold: First, in the business world especially, you have to have some time perspective to see the whole impact of a certain strategy. The full historical impact of a new product or service introduction is revealed only after significant time has passed. Second, my target readers are "first timers" to higher levels of leadership, and they may not be familiar with these tried-and-true examples and their long-term impact.

A second group of real-life examples comes from interviewing industry executives. And a third group of case studies are from my own experience.

Read on, then, for lots more information on innovation and the cultivation of new product ideas in the following chapters. I want you to experience the same adrenaline rush of walking into an unknown territory in your day job that I enjoy and thrive on in mine.

P.S. During a meeting, one of the boards I serve on stumbled on the "chicken and egg" dilemma cliché (for the gazillionth time in my career, I might add).

I jumped in without thinking and told the CEO, "Let's lay the egg and worry about selling the chicken later."

After that board meeting, I said to myself, "That could be a good title for a book." And so it was that what you're holding in your hand took root in my head.

ABBREVIATIONS AND ACRONYMS

AI	artificial intelligence
AIBO	artificial intelligence robot
B2B	business-to-business
B2C	business-to-consumer
CAD	computer-aided design
CAGR	compound annual growth rate
CDC	Centers for Disease Control and Prevention
CEO	chief executive officer
CFO	chief financial officer
CINO	chief innovation officer
CSC	consumer software customization
CTIO	chief technology innovation officer
CTO	chief technology officer
CVC	corporate venture capital
DSP	digital signal processor
EFFA	early field failure analysis (Apple Inc.)
EU	European Union
FAQs	frequently asked questions
FPGA	field-programmable gate array
G&A	general and administrative expenses
HNWI	high net worth individual
ICI	Imperial Chemical Industries
IoT	Internet of Things
IP	intellectual property
IPO	initial public offering
IPR	intellectual property rights
IRR	internal rate of return

IT	information technology
JIT	just in time
M&A	mergers and acquisitions
MG	minimum guarantee
NDA	nondisclosure agreement
NPV	net present value
NSF	National Science Foundation
P2P	peer-to-peer
PMI	Project Management Institute
PMP	Project Management Professional
PO	purchase order
PV	present value
R&D	research & development
ROBS	Rollovers as Business Start-ups
ROI	return on investment
SaaS	Software as a Service
SAM	serviceable available market
SBA	Small Business Administration
SEO	search engine optimization
TAM	total available market
UPA	United Productions of America
USPTO	U.S. Patent Office
VC	venture capital

PART I

FERTILIZE THE EGG

"Innovation is what distinguishes
between leaders and followers."

—Steve Jobs, former CEO of Apple Inc.

CHAPTER 1

WHY INNOVATE?

Humans are innovative. If we weren't, we would still be living in caves. The fact of life in the business world is that the ecosystem is in continuous flux. Consequently, you must innovate all the time to keep up with your customers' changing preferences and to outperform the competition. Simply put: Companies must adapt to market changes; otherwise, they will decline or die. Furthermore, if a company really wants to stay ahead, it must lead market change in order to force the competition to scramble in a catch-up mode or, better yet, to withdraw from the playing field because their products are obsolete. The convenient philosophy "if it ain't broke, don't fix it" doesn't work here, because if you do nothing and continue in a business-as-usual mode, eventually your competitors will force you to change, and it might be too late by then to recover.

Adapt to Market Changes—Or Die

In the 1960s, A&P was the largest grocery store chain in the United States. It went out of business in 2015. Why? It was too slow to respond to the changing competitive landscape in which other food retailers were opening larger and more modern supermarkets in response to customers' demands.[1]

The handwriting was on the wall in the 1970s. While other chains were moving to the suburbs to follow their customers, A&P seemed to be running five to ten years behind the migratory patterns of its own clientele. The Fortune 500's Top 10 performer of 1960 tried to reinvent itself, but A&P stores were outdated, and its efforts to combat high operating costs resulted in poor customer service. Labor costs were high, store volumes were low, and shoppers regarded the old buildings in shrinking urban areas as dirty, understocked, and overpriced.

In 1975, A&P hired outside management, which decided to close older stores and build modern ones. This was too little too late, however. When these efforts failed to turn the company around, it was sold to the Tengelmann Group of Germany. By 1981, A&P launched its second store-closing program, reducing the corporation to less than a thousand stores nationwide. The company continued to struggle. Zoom forward into the twenty-first century. The company's financial difficulties worsened so much during the 2008 recession it filed for Chapter 11 protection two years later. By that point, A&P had declined from its status as the nation's largest grocery retailer to being listed as twenty-eighth. The former food giant emerged briefly from bankruptcy in 2012 by becoming a private company with modest profitability. A&P had been for sale in 2013, but a suitable buyer could not be found. After declaring a loss in April

2015, it filed its second Chapter 11 bankruptcy paperwork that year. All its supermarkets were sold or closed by December 1, 2015.

It doesn't get much clearer than that. A company must adapt to market changes—that is, it must generate innovative ideas and create new products and services—or risk becoming defunct.

Product Innovation 101

A good product is one that solves people's needs.[2] (We all know that from introduction to marketing textbooks.) Humans need to eat, so invent food. People need to drink, so invent water. Individuals need to get from point A to point B, so invent a horse. So far, this is pretty basic stuff.

People want to communicate with their grandma, so you invent social media. What? Not so fast. Things are getting fuzzy now. The link between the need and the product is not so straightforward anymore. Nevertheless, the basic concept stays the same: Solve a problem.

The human mind needs to get more imaginative in the invention process to come up with a solution to problems. The road to the solution is twisted and convoluted these days. The common belief for a long time was that between your personal vehicle, your two legs, and different forms of traditional public transportation, all our transit needs were met. Uber came along in 2009, however, over a century after the invention of the automobile, and introduced a brand-new transportation approach—ridesharing. That's innovative problem-solving at its best. Uber addressed several problems in one solution: the rising cost of gasoline, parking problems in big cities, and the increasing number of motorists who were driving under the influence of drugs and alcohol, to name a few.

Lead Market Change—and Win

The Big Three U.S. automotive manufacturers, General Motors (NYSE: GM), Ford (NYSE: F), and Chrysler (2018's ticker NYSE: FCAU), were the undisputed suppliers of automobiles traversing America's asphalt highways and byways up to the early 1970s. Japanese automakers were faster than the Big Three, however, to respond to the 1970s oil crisis by designing and manufacturing smaller fuel-efficient vehicles. As a result, the U.S. market share of Japan's car manufacturers rose from 15 percent in the early 1970s to 27 percent in the early 1980s.[3]

Until the first OPEC oil embargo in 1973, automobile gas efficiency was a relatively unimportant issue to U.S. automakers and customers alike. After 1973, however, U.S. dealers were finding strong resistance to Detroit's full-size fuel-hungry offerings. Individual vehicle owners, realizing that the gas shortage was real, began trading in their traditional and problematic gas-guzzlers for smaller fuel-efficient Japanese vehicles that in those days were superior in quality as well.

The Big Three and other U.S. suppliers were in denial about this trend. Even up to the late 1970s, vehicle manufacturers didn't give serious thought to producing compact cars, with their attendant fuel efficiency. The big profits were in their traditional full-size vehicles.

One may argue that the Japanese suppliers happened to have the right product at the right time, which is true. If the U.S. automakers had reacted to the gasoline crisis faster, however, they might have minimized the success of their Japanese competitors on their home field.

Let's look at another example of leading market change—and winning. This time, the subject is a demographic shift in the overweight population and its impact on the food and beverage industry. The percentage of obese adults in the United States grew from 15 percent in 1990 to 36 percent at the turn of the twenty-first century.[4] As a result, the diet industry is booming. The number of Americans who consume diet foods and beverages grew from 78 million in 1986 to 187 million in 2010.[5]

Diet sodas first appeared in 1952, when Kirsch Bottling in Brooklyn, New York, launched a sugar-free drink called No-Cal. It was intended for diabetics, not for people trying to lose weight. Diet Rite, introduced in 1958, was the first low-calorie soda designed for weight control. Then, in 1962, Dr Pepper released a diet version of its soft drink. Its market acceptance was slow because of the misconception that it was meant for diabetics.

A year later, The Coca-Cola Company joined the diet soft drink market by launching Tab, which was a huge success. Pepsi released Patio Diet Cola in 1963 and renamed it Diet Pepsi the following year. Diet 7 Up was released that same year under the name Like. It was discontinued in 1969 due to the U.S. government ban of cyclamate sweetener. After reformulation, it was reintroduced as Diet 7 Up in 1970 and went through several rebrandings over the years. Coca-Cola countered by releasing Diet Coke in 1982 because consumers more easily identified it as a Coca-Cola product than their previous Tab brand had.

Sales of sugar-free, zero-calorie, and "lite" beverages have skyrocketed ever since. Today, the diet soda segment accounts for about 20 percent of the total soda consumption in the United States. I'd say that these leaders of market change are winning big time, wouldn't you?[6]

We shall see repeated in other case studies these same two common phenomena: One, Often a product enjoys a level of success its originators had not anticipated or intended when they launched it; and two, the first one to market does not always win the race. Once consumers validate an early entry in the marketplace, a big gorilla incumbent will enter the race and push the market toward a big success. This was the case with diet sodas as well as personal computers.

One of the early players in the personal computers space was Commodore. IBM entered the game late, but for a while became the biggest player. (Commodore 64s and other vintage models sell today on eBay.) It's the same with electrical cars. Tesla was the first to market, and only after Tesla showed some traction did all the big players introduce their own brand of electric vehicle.

Evolve with the Ecosystem

We all experience the interrelationships between software and hardware with our personal computers and smart phones. New generations of faster and more powerful processors have been released very frequently in recent years. The additional improved hardware performance allows the software suppliers to add more functionality to each next release. If you are like me and don't rush to buy every latest computer or smart phone model du jour, you nevertheless will find yourself being forced to change hardware every few years because your older hardware can't keep up with the latest software releases anymore. This is one example of how a technology change in one part of the ecosystem drives follow-up technology changes in other areas. As stated earlier in the context of adapting to market change, this is an ongoing phenomenon. Simply put, evolve or die.

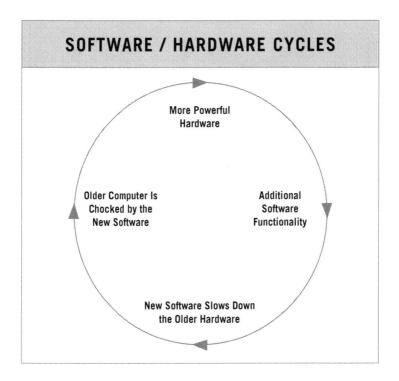

SOFTWARE / HARDWARE CYCLES

More Powerful
Hardware

Older Computer Is
Chocked by the
New Software

Additional
Software
Functionality

New Software Slows Down
the Older Hardware

One MIT study compared the number of new products introduced in different categories between 1980 and 1998. The categories were cereal, ice cream, spices, deodorizers, paper towels, milk,
coffee, and beer. In all categories, the number of new products
introduced in 1998 was significantly higher than the number of
new products introduced in 1980 by as much as six to ten times.
This study demonstrates the constant need for ongoing innovation
to keep pace with the market, to evolve with the ecosystem.[7]

Another way to look at the faster pace of corporations'
lives today is the average life span of S&P companies, which
dropped from a range of thirty to sixty years in the 1960s to a
range of fifteen to twenty years in the first decade and a half of
the twenty-first century.[8]

The evolution in market situations is also demonstrated clearly by looking at changes in Fortune 500 lists over time. The list on the following page focuses only on the top ten global players.

1960 Fortune 500 – Top 10		2017 Fortune 500 – Top 10	
AT&T	U.S.	Walmart	U.S.
GM	U.S.	State Grid	China
Standard Oil	U.S.	Sinopec	China
Ford	U.S.	China National Petrol	China
Shell	E.U.	Toyota	Japan
A&P	U.S.	VW	E.U.
GE	U.S.	Shell	E.U.
Sears	U.S.	Berkshire Hathaway	U.S.
Unilever	E.U.	Apple	U.S.
U.S. Steel	U.S.	Exxon Mobil	U.S.

Note these dramatic observations in particular:
- Nine out of the top ten for 1960 are not in the top ten for 2017.
- In 1960, eight were U.S. based and two European. In 2017, only four were U.S. based, three Chinese, two European, and one Japanese.

Here are a few other observations:
- No consumer electronics corporations made it onto the 1960 list, and only Apple made it onto the 2017 list.

- Speaking of Apple, it started as a personal computer company, the little niche player nipping at the heels of the large computer suppliers, mainly IBM. But with the transition to entertainment and smartphones, Apple became the giant they are today, surpassing IBM by a country mile.

- GM and Ford were the only car manufacturers on the 1960 list, but they're not on the 2017 roster, having been replaced by VW and Toyota as Fortune 500 Top 10ers.

- The only company that survived both lists is the oil giant Shell.

Here's another example of how one technology change drives another, this time in the bathroom.[9] Until the end of the nineteenth century, people used old newspapers and catalogues as toilet paper. It was recycling at its finest. Off-the-shelf commercial toilet papers existed in the market, but most people couldn't justify spending money for something they could get free of charge. (Millennials: Be advised that there was no Internet in those days, and most people got their news, business opportunities, and coupons by subscribing to paper-based newspapers and magazines, often more than one.) The main places you would find toilet paper were hotels.

The widespread acceptance of the product didn't officially occur until a new technology demanded it. By the turn of the twentieth century, more and more homes were being built with flush toilets connected to indoor plumbing systems. This new technology required a product that could be flushed away with minimal damage to the pipes; old newspapers could no longer cut it. In no time, toilet paper ads boasted that the product was recommended both by doctors and by plumbers!

Takeaways

- Lead market change and watch your competitors scurry to catch up to your sales figures.

- Adapt to market changes (has your customer base literally moved?) or risk failing or fading away.

- Evolve and drive your product sales ever higher in the business ecosystem by creating new versions of them.

- Assume that your competitors are working on something that might kill your business. You must *continuously* innovate to keep the edge—and stay alive.

CHAPTER 2

THE INNOVATIVE MIND-SET

It can be quite daunting to jump-start the process of generating ideas for new products or services. This is especially true if you're a first-time CEO whose career up to this point has been strictly in marketing or finance or manufacturing or any other organizational discipline. Now you'll be meeting with team members from those and other departments to maximize everyone's thoughts and energies. This chapter opens with insights about how to draw the best ideas from your innovation team and personnel, underscoring the importance of diversity over homogeneity in the team membership. The second half of the chapter helps you get a grasp on the numerous types of business innovation you and your team should consider so your efforts are well targeted from the start. (In chapter 3, you'll learn about key sources you can research or interact with as you search for innovative ideas to pursue.)

Ideation Design and Facilitation

Companies can enhance the creativity of their employees by taking them through structured ideation sessions. Ideation is generally defined as the creative process of generating, developing, and communicating new ideas. The specifics of the process may change depending on the type of new ideas the group is looking for. Let's review a couple of techniques.

I listened to a podcast about two of these techniques developed by thought leader and creative thinker Bryan Mattimore. One of them he calls brainwriting and the other brainwalking.[1] They are both similar to brainstorming, but they've been modified for the innovation process. They both also start with presenting the creative challenge to the team.

In brainwriting, each participant receives a piece of paper and writes down an idea for meeting the challenge. She then passes the paper to the next person, who then builds on that idea or uses it as a stimulus to trigger a new idea. The papers are usually passed for four to five rounds. After the final round, each sheet is returned to its originator, who then circles one or two favorite ideas to discuss and build on with the group as a whole. This technique gets around the introvert/extrovert problem in a traditional brainstorming session.

Conceptually, brainwalking is very similar to brainwriting, but it involves moving the people instead of the papers. The brainwalking session starts by taping large blank sheets of flip chart paper on the walls around the room, which are called "ideation stations." The first person goes to an ideation station and writes an idea at the top of the paper. Next, he rotates to his neighbor's paper and adds an idea, just as he had done in the brainwriting exercise. After five rotations, each person returns to their original sheet and circles one or two of their favorite ideas. The act of getting people up and moving increases the energy in the room significantly. Also, the ideas in brainwalking, unlike those in brainwriting, are made public, which is a benefit in an ideation session. Why? Because it's affirming and encouraging the participants to see dozens of ideas on the walls after only a few minutes of work.

Seeing all the ideas on the wall also creates a sense of shared purpose and group identity, which can help later in the process. And, as you'll see in the next section, it reinforces the value of having a mix of participants of different ages, life experiences, work histories, and backgrounds among the ideation teams.

Innovation and Diversity

Back in the 1980s, diversity became popular as a social equal opportunity subject. Fast-forward twenty to thirty years, and it has been proven that diversity is indeed good for business: especially for businesses, especially when it comes to innovation. Innovation is all about thinking outside the box. When a group is homogeneous, their collective boxes are very similar; thus, as a team, they don't add much to each other's thinking. In the case of a diverse group, the individual boxes are set apart from each other; thus, the collective team box is much broader, and potentially covers more possibilities. The following chart demonstrates this reasoning.

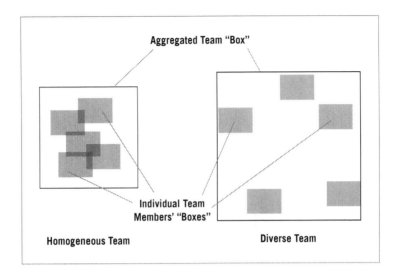

In research on diversity conducted in 2013 by *Harvard Business Review*, staff surveyed 1,800 professionals, reviewed 40 case studies, and held numerous focus groups and interviews. The research team identified two kinds of diversity: inherent and acquired. Inherent diversity involves traits an individual is born with, such as gender, ethnicity, and sexual orientation. Acquired diversity involves traits one gains from experience, such as from different schools, working in another country, various companies worked for, military background, and so on.[2]

Companies whose leadership team exhibits at least three inherent and three acquired diversity traits were defined as having two-dimensional diversity or, as the researchers nicknamed it, 2-D diversity.

By correlating diversity in leadership with market outcomes, they learned that companies with 2-D diversity out-innovate and outperform others. The metrics were related to market share gains, and the respondents reported 45 to

70 percent better market share results than did companies that lacked 2-D diversity.

First Round Capital, a venture capital (VC) firm based in the Bay Area, followed 200 start-up companies over a ten-year period. One finding from their research was that companies with at least one female founder performed 63 percent better than did companies with all-male founding teams.[3]

A diversity mind-set doesn't have to lead to compromised hiring; rather, it "adds points" to candidates who will bring diversity into the group. In other words, I am not suggesting that you hire a candidate just because he or she adds diversity to the team. Hire based on a qualified candidate's skill sets, but also factor in that diversity adds value on top of all those other skills.

People are tribal and tend to gravitate to people like themselves. In the "old days," hiring managers felt more comfortable hiring people like themselves, thus creating redundancy in the team. Today, it is pretty common knowledge that diversity contributes to overall team performance, and hiring managers should value diverse candidates as an added value to the team.

Diversity is easy to accomplish in a large company purely because the large number of employees creates more opportunities to hire a variety of people with different backgrounds. Furthermore, diversity candidates will feel more comfortable joining an employer that already has "people like them." An early-stage start-up with just a handful of people may have a hard time achieving diversity in the core team. One way a small start-up can overcome the lack of diversity is by hiring a few diverse advisers or consultants to attend only strategic meetings that require out-of-the box creativity. As the start-up grows, it will create more opportunities to hire diverse employees.

The other challenge within diverse teams is to create an environment of nonjudgmental brainstorming so that people with nontraditional or nonconventional thinking will not be reluctant to voice their opinions.

Types of Innovation in Business

The purpose of this section is to explain the different types of innovations any company can undertake. Too many people (especially engineers) think about business innovation in terms of product innovation. This section stretches that idea to cover many additional innovation opportunities.

The dictionary definition of "innovation" is "introducing something new." In the realm of business, you'll find these different ways of introducing that "something new."

- *Business Model Innovation* refers to the creation, or reinvention, of a business model. (Example: Introduce a flat monthly subscription instead of charging by the hour or by the issue.) In chapter 7, you'll read much more about the two main types of business model and their related spin-offs.

- *Cost Reduction Innovation* is about finding a way to build the same product or provide the same service for a lower cost. (Example: Move the company's call center overseas.)

- *Disruptive Innovation* creates a new market category. (Example: The introduction of the first personal computers or the introduction of the first automobile.)

- *Eco-Innovation* is a term used to describe products and processes that contribute to saving environmental resources such as energy or water. (Example: Produce better building insulation that saves HVAC energy consumption.)

- *Experience Innovation* tries to create holistic experiences by emotionally engaging consumers. (Example: Movie theaters providing full food service to their guests at their seats while they watch a show or salons serving a glass of wine to patrons while they wait for their hairdresser.)

- *Incremental Innovation* improves existing products and services. (Example: Add a new feature to an automobile, such as safety cameras or better headlights.) (See the box titled "A Cautionary Tale: Corporate Cannibalism and Market Cannibalism" in chapter 3 for more details on when best to pursue this type of business innovation.)

- *Process Innovation* is the implementation of a new or significantly improved production or delivery method. (Example: The introduction of a production line by Ford Motor Company.)

- *Service Innovation* can be defined as improving customer interaction channels. (Example: Offer the option of making reservations online to improve and expedite the processs previously done only by phone.)

- *Supply Chain Innovation* is about applying different ways to improve your own supply chain in order to reduce cycle time, cost, wait times, and so on. (Example: Michael Dell started Dell Computers to configure personal computers for mail order customers by mixing and matching subsystems from different suppliers.)

All these types of innovation in business are not alternatives to one another; rather, they are multiple types that can be used together. As you read in the introduction, Toyota implements two innovations per minute, and those are reflected within all the innovation types described previously. Chapter 3, "Where to Look for Ideas for Innovations," describes in more detail how to evaluate different innovative ideas. When your resources are limited, prioritize the innovation ideas you came up with and choose the ones that will have the most positive impact on the business.

Takeaways

- Use brainwriting and brainwalking to trigger your innovation team's ideas.

- Mix it up! The more diverse the team, the more imaginative and far-reaching your company's ideas—and, ultimately, products—will be.

- Don't get stuck with a narrow definition and mind-set about business innovation. At least nine varieties are listed here for you to choose from.

- Hiring diverse candidates is just the beginning. The other part of the equation is to create a working environment that will encourage people with different opinions to speak up without being criticized.

PART II

LAY THE EGG

"If I had asked my customers what they wanted,
they would have said a faster horse."

—Henry Ford

CHAPTER 3

WHERE TO LOOK FOR IDEAS FOR THE EGG

The critical question every product or service innovation team must ask and answer with certainty is this: Which egg will produce the best chicken? And the ideas for business innovation the team will consider can come from a number of different sources. These vary from a company's customers themselves, from corporate venture capitalists, employees, and from academia. In other cases, the innovation team might have a germ of an idea already, but it could only be feasible if they were to partner with another source. Let's have a look at each of these potential idea funnels and see how, historically, they have contributed to some of the most recognized names in the marketplace.

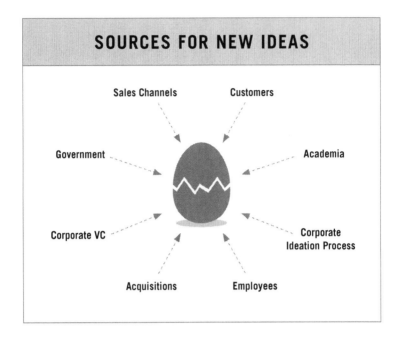

SOURCES FOR NEW IDEAS

Sales Channels Customers

Government Academia

Corporate VC Corporate Ideation Process

Acquisitions Employees

Customer-Driven Ideas

Customers reveal a need, and in response, suppliers come up with a solution to fulfill it. More often than not, customers don't specify what they envision the solution to be. They expect you to solve the problem. If, for example, the customer complains that the reception area in your office is too cold, your solution in winter may be to turn on or up the heat or to provide the people in the waiting area with a blanket. Or, if it's a hot summer day, just increase the air conditioner thermostat threshold so the room isn't so chilly.

When the customer does offer a solution, it is always a good idea to ask her what problem she is trying to solve. When you start a dialogue about the problem, this discussion may lead to a better solution than the one the customer had originally thought about. Just be careful not to put customers in a position in which they will react emotionally and defend the solution she proposed originally.

Here are few real-life examples that illustrate the customer-driven generation of ideas.

When a massive number of Russian Jews immigrated to Israel during the 1990s, it created a need for transportation between the two countries. Russian family members began to visit their relatives in Israel, and Russian-Israelis went back to Russia to visit relatives who had stayed behind. In 1990, both El-Al and Aeroflot launched service between Moscow and Tel-Aviv to cater to this need. A straightforward, simple innovation.

Young people all over the world love to listen to music. In the late 1970s, Akio Morita, cofounder of Sony, knew it very well because he had a teenage daughter in the house as well as many young engineers in the office.[1] At that point in time, Sony was already a consumer electronics powerhouse. The question for Sony was, is there a way to link those two realities with a new product?

First they looked at the U.S. and Japanese markets. Americans for the most part commute to work in their personal car and listen to music on their car radio. Most Japanese, however (even the wealthier ones), commute to the office via public trains and subways. The state-of-the-art smallest tape recorder in those days was notebook size and too heavy to carry around as a portable device. People mainly used tape recorders to record music from the radio or other devices and as a home entertainment system. That's why they had built-in loudspeakers.

Next, as Morita-san and Sony's other cofounder, Ibuka-san,

discussed the problem, they realized that a portable device needed neither all the recording circuitry nor the loudspeakers of a tape recorder. Removing these two functions from the device allowed them to reduce it from a shoulder-mounted tape recorder to pocket size, and in 1979 the Walkman was born and became an overnight hit all over the world.

The California Gold Rush during the 1850s created a significant gender imbalance since most of the gold miners were males. In fact, 90 percent of the population in that Wild West territory was male. (The gap was eventually closed, but it took about a hundred years to achieve gender balance. The first census to show an equal number of males and females in the State of California was in 1950!)[2] This gap resulted in a migration of women to serve that male population hungry for the female touch in their lives. Women flooded to California from several U.S. cities and even other countries to work as prostitutes and entertainers and thus capitalize on the scarcity of females among the gold miners. Many of these women ended up staying and marrying miners. Some of the ladies became so prosperous and powerful that they helped keep the local community services, such as law enforcement, doctors, churches, and politicians, in business.

This phenomenon was a spontaneous response to market need, without any organized innovation process behind it.

Innovating for B2B Customers

In B2B (Business-to-Business) cases, it is common for the customer to specify the solution and ask suppliers to bid on it. When the customer is large enough, this one single opportunity could justify the whole development project, thus significantly reducing the market adoption risk.

While I served as product planning manager for Motorola's Microcontrollers business unit, I led the process of selecting and bidding on customer-defined products. At the time, we had several pretty popular platforms that customers liked, and we were blessed with several household-name blue chip customers. These customers would ask for additions or modifications to the standard platform to optimize the product for their particular application. Due to the size of these customers, each such project had a rapid ramping up to market launch because it fit right into an existing high-volume product our customers already had. This fueled our growth from $300 million to more than $2 billion in less than ten years. Obviously, we worked jointly with the customers to develop the specifications for these customer-driven products. Each product had its own story, but that is beyond the scope of this section.

Poultry powerhouse Sanderson Farms Inc. (NASDAQ: SAFM) has benefited from a similar product planning process. When I interviewed the company's CFO, Mike Cockrell, he explained that Sanderson Farms grew from a revenue of $100 million in 1982 to better than $3 billion in 2017. When you go to the company's website, all you will find listed are pretty generic chicken products packaged in different ways and in different combinations of chicken parts. What drives their successful growth strategy, in part, has been their partnering with high-volume business customers, such as large restaurant chains, to create particular products prepared to their specification. This creates an exceedingly high growth path with relatively low market risk.

Remember, however, the importance of making these B2B customer discussions a two-way brainstorm and dialogue about each customer's needs. Have the customers articulate the problem they want to solve, but avoid—at least initially—defining a solution. Instead, brainstorm about alternatives and the pros and cons of different options that they and you have proposed.

Corporate-Sponsored Innovative Ideas

Very large companies often suffer from a slower decision-making process, which slows down their innovation execution accordingly. Many of these companies recognize this issue and implement methodologies and processes to compensate for that sluggishness. Two such examples are Tata and ARAMCO.

Tata Group Innovation Forum Case Study

Tata Group is a $100 billion global conglomerate based in India, with over 600,000 employees worldwide. Its businesses range from automobiles, hospitality, and energy to health, IT, and many more. Tata Group is trying to leverage its size and diversity to be a catalyst for innovation. To that end, it created the Tata Group Innovation Forum (TGIF), a network that connects Tata companies all over the world, stimulates innovative thinking, and fosters collaboration and research between the diverse managers from the Tata companies from various industries.

TGIF organizes a number of events and workshops and facilitates interaction among Tata executives, outside innovation experts, and academics.[3] It regularly invites academics and other specialists in the field to conduct workshops and seminars that introduce new innovation concepts and tools and stimulate pioneering thinking among its executives. The group has set up several platforms for collaboration on technology and innovation both within the Tata ecosystem as well as with external organizations.

TGIF brings together technologists and researchers from different Tata companies so that these sister companies learn from each other by sharing their research and technology road maps, infrastructure, skills, and competencies. Subsequently, clusters have been formed within TGIF, which are working on collaborative projects, leveraging the extensive variety within the forum as a whole. (Recall the section titled "Innovation and Diversity" in chapter 2 that discusses the value of such variety in generating new ideas.)

ARAMCO Case Study

ARAMCO, Saudi Arabia's national oil company, is another example of a megacompany that has diversified into other industries. ARAMCO has been the number one oil company in the world, with revenue in excess of $350 billion, making it the second-largest company overall after Walmart.[4] Until the end of the twentieth century, ARAMCO's focus was entirely on oil exploration, refining, and shipping. After the year 2000, the company realized that in order to survive in the long term it must expand and diversify. Unlike Tata Group, which diversified into other industries, ARAMCO chose to expand into adjacent areas in their ecosystem. It created global research centers in energy and technology hubs around the world such as Scotland, China, several U.S. locations, South Korea, the Netherlands,

France, and of course Saudi Arabia. It also created its own corporate VC arm, Saudi Aramco Energy Ventures.[5]

For example, ARAMCO started to invest in automotive fuel efficiency, petrochemicals, seismic modeling, robotics, and renewable energy, to name just a few. The R&D team at ARAMCO Research Center in Detroit, Michigan, for instance, focuses on competitive transportation solutions, improving the efficiency of current and future engines, and reducing the overall environmental impact, cost, and complexity of engine systems. The center accommodates light-duty and heavy-duty fuels research programs and also offers full on-site integration and the demonstration of new vehicle technologies. The Strategic Transportation Analysis Team, based there, provides dynamic industry analysis relevant to fuels.

Another expansion is into petrochemicals. ARAMCO entered into a joint venture with the German specialty chemicals company LANXESS. The new company, Arlanxeo, is a world leader in the development, production, marketing, sale, and distribution of synthetic rubber and elastomers used in the global tire industry, auto parts manufacturing, construction, and oil and gas industries. The joint venture helped unlock the full economic potential of the Saudi's hydrocarbon resources.

The previous two examples show how large corporations can stimulate innovation and turn their bloated size from a disadvantage into an advantage.

Academic Research–Driven Ideas

The role of universities is twofold: One, they expand human knowledge, and two, they teach future professionals. When expanding knowledge is a main goal, the commercial viability of these expansions is not always fully understood, nor is it a priority. Often, the opposite is the case. The newly discovered knowledge could facilitate new commercial products, however. Universities know that, and many of them have a commercialization office whose charter is to take the studies from the academic tower to the street. This activity is a moneymaker for many universities because they collect royalties from the commercial use of their intellectual properties. Likewise, industries recognize that the universities could be a source of innovation, and many large corporations have created a university relations process to capture the relevant inventions for their business (before their competitors will).

Universities can augment their funding sources by working with the industry. This relationship has become an increasingly important consideration in most countries as government backing for higher education has become scarce. University administrators feel the pressure to supplement their institution's funding by various means, one of which is sponsored research. For example, MIT made $50 million from intellectual property licensing in 2017.[6] Working with the industry also provides pedagogical and academic value for the students and faculty: Both groups keep up with the practical problems in the real world and gain access to knowledge developed outside academia. This is particularly important in many emerging fields where academic research and publication often lag behind industry.

University-industry collaboration can take several forms. For example, the National Science Foundation in the United States identifies four interrelated components in the university-industry relationship: research support, cooperative research, knowledge transfer, and technology transfer. My favorite part of these relationships was the students' internships. These young minds come to work for you during the summer, not having preconceived boundaries to block their creativity. They always make innovative contributions by asking out-of-the-box questions.

Schlumberger Limited's Story

Schlumberger Limited (NYSE:SLB) is one of many companies that recognize the innovation potential inherent in partnering with universities. Schlumberger provides the global oil and gas industry with the technology for reservoir characterization, drilling, production, and processing. The company works in more than eighty-five countries and employs approximately 100,000 people, who represent better than 140 nationalities. According to Dr. Najib Abusalbi, its director of corporate university relations, Schlumberger has recently engaged in research and engineering collaborations with more than seventy universities worldwide. Their six global research centers are strategically located next to major universities.

Schlumberger's Corporate Science and Technology Committee periodically recommends which areas to focus on in the company's search for new technologies. The University Relations team will then identify key universities that are known leaders of knowledge and research in those key areas; review the research these universities are currently conducting in those domains; and suggest ideas for additional research projects. The joint research activities are then conducted in several ways:

- University professors or post docs spend time working at Schlumberger research and engineering centers.

- Schlumberger funds specific university projects.

- Joint projects are undertaken between universities' personnel and Schlumberger engineers and/or scientists.

Schlumberger is also active with the National Center for Entrepreneurship and Technology Transfer.

The University of Texas–Austin's Innovation Center

Louise Epstein is the managing director of the Innovation Center of the University of Texas–Austin's Cockrell School of Engineering. She explained that the center helps professors bridge the academic-corporate gap and take results of their academic research to the next stepping-stone on the path to commercialization. Professors who feel that their research has commercial prospects apply for the program. If selected, they get a small budget of $5,000 to $50,000 from the university, entrepreneurship mentoring, and engagement with business executives who help manage the process. The selected professors are also engaged with the National Science Foundation (NSF) I-Corps program, which prepares scientists and engineers to extend their focus beyond the university laboratory and accelerates the economic and societal benefits of NSF-funded, basic research projects that are ready to move toward commercialization. The general idea is to inject some business sense into otherwise strictly science- and engineering-focused professors through the NSF I-Corps program's boot camp entrepreneurship training.

Corporate Venture Capitalists Scout for Ideas

Many corporations have realized in recent years that the start-up community is initiating significant innovations, so those corporations have launched their own VC arms. This new type of venture capitalism is called corporate venture capital (CVC). Most CVC departments seek to identify and exploit strategic synergies between themselves and the new ventures. A CVC department does not generate the ideas for innovative products/services itself; rather, by looking to invest in new companies, it attracts entrepreneurs to apply for funding, which in turn supplies the CVC department's parent corporation with a stream of ideas.

The goal is to benefit from the additional growth potential contributed by the start-ups. For instance, investing firms may want to obtain a window on new technologies, to enter new markets, to identify acquisition targets, and/or to access new resources.

Less common are financially driven CVC investments where parent firms are looking for leverage on returns, much like any normal VC.

This CVC process is a win-win for the start-up, which stands to benefit in two key ways: One, the investing corporation might be a potential customer; and two, the investing corporation might be a potential route for an exit should it acquire the start-up. Some entrepreneurs avoid this route, however, because they fear that the strategic CVC will limit their freedom and funnel them through a narrow path that the CVC needs. Similarly, they fear that the CVC will not allow them to address other customers that might be competitors of the investing corporations.

Some of the early entries into the CVC world were Intel, Nokia, and Cisco. Today, it has become almost a must-have function in any corporation that requires a constant flow of innovations to survive.

Samsung Ventures' Story

Samsung Ventures, founded in 1999, is based in Seoul, South Korea, but has offices in many technology centers around the globe. Per my recent conversation with Ori Kirshner, head of Samsung VC Israel, its areas of interest are semiconductors, IT, software, Internet services, biotechnology, contents business, and more. Although most of their investments are made at a later stage, Series C and higher, exceptions have been made on a case-by-case basis. One of the important criteria, rightly so, is buy-in by the relevant business unit inside Samsung (KRX:005930). The business unit knows their needs better than anyone; thus, they are an important part of the selection process. They also look for an ongoing cooperation between the sponsoring business unit and the start-up. Their portfolio includes dozens of start-ups in different stages. In addition to Samsung Ventures, which focuses on Samsung's strategic investments, the company has two independent VCs: Samsung Next, which focuses on early-stage software and services, and Catalyst, which invests in early-stage start-ups with groundbreaking, disruptive ideas in areas such as artificial intelligence (AI), Internet of Things (IoT), smart machines, Cloud infrastructure, digital health technology, and device technology.[7]

Tyson Ventures' Story

As part of its commitment to innovation and growth, Tyson Foods, Inc. (NYSE:TSN) has launched a VC fund called Tyson Ventures with $150 million that will be invested in companies developing breakthrough technologies, business models, and products to sustainably feed a growing world population.[8] The fund is targeted to complement the company's continuing investment in innovation in its core fresh meats, poultry, and prepared foods businesses. The fund will concentrate on two investment pillars:

1. **Sustainability:** Companies that focus on reducing food waste, increasing food security, addressing food deserts throughout the world, and finding alternative proteins.

2. **The Internet of Food:** Companies that operate as e-commerce models, direct-to-consumer businesses, sensor technologies, and data analytics around consumer purchasing trends.

Tyson Ventures collaborates with food entrepreneurs who are pioneering new products and technology that are making meaningful changes and improvement to food ecosystems.

Mature External Partnering Prospects

In some cases, the company will acquire a full-grown chicken: That is, it acquires access to a mature product rather than develops one. The reasons a company takes this partnering approach could be any or all of the following:

1. They prefer to let the market decide which idea is valid.

2. They prefer to let other entities take the risk to invest in developing the new idea.

3. They have a new product that is cost-effective only in one market segment but not cost-effective in a more price-sensitive vertical until driven further down its learning curve.

4. They have had a change in strategy that requires entrance into a new products category or a new market segment.

In the following section, we will review a few sources to acquire a relatively mature product.

Acquisitions

Once a company decides to enter a new product or service category, one option is to develop it in-house. An alternative strategy, however, is to acquire another company or a portion of a company that already has that business. The advantage of doing this is to save development time and reduce the technology and development risks.

Let's look at a company that did just that.

Intel/McAfee's Story

In 2009, Intel realized that cyber security was becoming a major component of an overall solution their customers required.[9] Up to that point, customers bought the microprocessor technology from suppliers such as Intel or ARM and then integrated it with security software from other suppliers. Intel (NASDAQ: INTC) wanted to be able to offer its customers a one-stop shop for the chip technology together with its security, and so it acquired one of the leading suppliers of security software, McAfee, for $7.68 billion. Otherwise, had they not acquired McAfee, Intel would have had to hire hundreds of engineers to develop the security software themselves, which could have cost them $5 to $10 billion, and entering the market three years later, carrying all the technology and execution risks on their shoulders. Acquiring one of the existing players was the right move on their part.

Government Applications

One of the issues with new products, especially hi-tech ones, is the prohibitive cost of early prototypes. (We will talk about this issue at length in the discussion about learning curves in chapter 16.) Here let me just say that governments are a good launch pad for new technologies because they are, for the most part, less cost-sensitive than the day-to-day commercial markets are. This allows governments to pioneer new technologies even when they are too expensive for day-to-day commercial use and lets the government's application drive down the learning curve to a more affordable point for civilian use. One such example is the "colonoscopy pill" (official name PillCam).

The PillCam Case Study

The PillCam capsule endoscopy platform uses miniature visualization technology to produce clear images of the esophagus, stomach, small bowel, and colon. The patient swallows the capsule as though it were a normal pill. The PillCam travels through the patient's digestive system and transmits the pictures wirelessly to the specialist's computer. The physician tracks its progress through the patient's digestive system to look for any abnormalities, to monitor disease activity, and to assess treatment efficacy.

The PillCam was originally developed in 1998 by Dr. Gabi Iddan and Dr. Gavriel Meron, cofounders of Given Imaging, a start-up based in Israel. Elron Electronic Industries—Israel's leading technology holding company—provided initial funding for the company, in cooperation with Rafael Advanced Defense Systems. The idea for the product came to Dr. Iddan while he was working for the Israeli government; he envisioned that the miniaturized visualization technology they had developed for a government application could be applied for medical use as well. The PillCam capsule uses a radio developed by Zarlink Semiconductor Limited's medical teams in San Diego, California, and in Järfälla, Sweden. (Microsemi acquired Zarlink in 2011.) In 2004, the U.S. Food and Drug Administration as well as the European Union (EU) approved the PillCam. In 2014, Covidien, an Irish-based medical technology firm, acquired Given Imaging for $870 million. A short year later, Medtronic, Inc. (NYSE:MDT) acquired Covidien for $42.9 billion.

This PillCam story demonstrates the value of government applications on a couple of levels. First, the military government application drove the cost of a miniature camera down to where it was picked up for a commercial use. Second, it demonstrates how a larger company (Covidian) gets its hands around innovation by acquiring another company that owns an innovative technology.

A Cautionary Tale: Corporate Cannibalism and Market Cannibalism

Corporate cannibalism occurs when companies introduce new products into a market where they have already established previous generations of these products. In effect, the new products are competing against their own incumbent products.

Cannibalism will happen anytime a company introduces a new generation of products that will replace their previous one. Whenever Apple introduces iPhone model X+1, for instance, it will cannibalize iPhone model X. This is a necessary evil that companies must nevertheless endure, because if you avoid introducing a new generation for fear of cannibalizing your own products, guess what will happen? Your competitors will do it. The trick is to wean customers off the earlier generation onto next-generation products without losing them to the next-generation products of your competitors.

Constructive cannibalism, or *constructive phase-over*, is a situation in which the combination of the added sales from the new products plus the declined sales and profits from the old generation will still generate a better and greater overall top-line revenue and bottom-line profit.

Destructive cannibalism, or *destructive phase-over*, is a situation where the older-generation business declines faster than the new-generation growth. This may happen in two cases: One, the existing customers replace the older-generation product being phased out with a competitor's new-generation product. Two, the company drops the price of the older-generation product too aggressively. The result is that lower unit sales multiplied by the lower unit price will create too big a void that the sales of the newly introduced generation of products will not grow fast enough to compensate for.

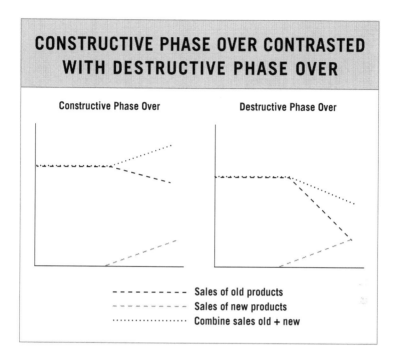

CONSTRUCTIVE PHASE OVER CONTRASTED WITH DESTRUCTIVE PHASE OVER

Constructive Phase Over   Destructive Phase Over

- - - - - - - - - - Sales of old products
~ ~ ~ ~ ~ ~ ~ ~ Sales of new products
· · · · · · · · · · · · · · · · Combine sales old + new

There may be a case of *unintentional cannibalism,* or *political canni-balism.* This occurs when the new product is assigned to one business unit while the old product is still managed by another business unit. In situations like these, there is a risk that the two business units will start to compete against each other, which may compromise the overall financial performance of the parent company. For example: The manager of the old business unit will start to compete on price in order to not lose customers to his colleague from the new product business unit. This may create a price war between the two business units.

The company can address this problem in one of two ways: One, assign the new product to the same business unit that is managing the old product. Two, create an incentive plan that will encourage the manager of the older product to phase out in an orderly manner, plus maybe get some extra bonus points from the success of the new product introduction.

Takeaways

- Innovation can be seeded by multiple sources: customers, academia, government, CVC departments, employees, partners, and so on. Take advantage of all the potential sources available to you, and furthermore, create processes to encourage these sources to communicate their innovation ideas.

- The innovation idea must fulfill a real customer need, and the solution to the need must come in an acceptable price to the market and provide an acceptable profit to the supplier.

- In the case of an evolutionary product, the phase over must be managed carefully to avoid destructive cannibalism.

CHAPTER 4

EVALUATING NEW PRODUCT IDEAS

As discussed in the previous chapter, innovation ideas come from multiple sources. Often, the company faces the dilemma of having more ideas than resources to implement them. When that's the case, the innovation process must include prioritization and elimination cycles to filter out only the highest-priority ideas that will then move into the implementation process.

When it comes to realistically evaluating a new product or service idea, bear in mind these two key rules.

Rule One: A new product must fulfill a market need (at launch time).[1]

Rule Two: The predicted return on investment (ROI) must show a positive outcome.[2] ("Positive" could mean different things in different cases. See more about it in the "Finance" section later in the chapter.)

When you face the need to eliminate some ideas, the questions to ask are these:

In the case of Rule One: How painful is the need? What are the alternatives the market has today and/or what is likely to be available in the near future?

In the case of Rule Two: Do the pure math. Just quantify the revenue potential and the profit potential of each idea, and compare it to the investment needed to implement it.

Keep reading for more about the prioritization checklist.

When you are a start-up, you normally address one specific need with one solution, and thus the discussion is a simple single-dimension equation. In the world of large corporations, however, additional considerations must be taken into account—even when your answer to whether or not your innovation meets Rule One and Rule Two is yes. Those considerations constitute another key rule:

Rule Three: The devil is in the details.

A proper new product evaluation process must have a checklist that factors in all the details that are relevant to the business. Six of these "devilish" details are reviewed at length in this chapter: strategy, R&D, manufacturing and supply chain, market channels, organization, and finance. But first, let's look at a tool I've written for teams to use as they evaluate their innovative ideas.

New Idea Evaluation Checklist

Once you run into a good new idea, you may want to check its feasibility by going through the following checklist before spending too much time and money on it. In other words, this is an evaluation go/no-go gate to use in assessing which idea is practically doable and which presents too many obstacles. This checklist is another way to help you identify—and address—all the disciplines involved in the innovation process.

1. **How do people solve this problem today?** Or is it possible the status quo is good enough? Remember: People are normally resistive to change. Your new idea needs to be significantly appealing to break through the status quo.

2. **Are the basic technology building blocks available today?** Or do you need to conduct additional technology research to facilitate developing the product (which will add significant budget and schedule risk to the program)? A breakthrough product doesn't necessarily need a breakthrough technology.

3. **What is the total available market (TAM)?** What is the serviceable available market (SAM)? What is the market share that's expected to be captured?

Let's say you invent a new type of athletic shoe. The TAM is all the people in the world who participate in sports. If the new invention is mostly relevant for French tennis players between the ages of twenty-five and fifty, the SAM will be the number of French tennis players in that age group. The tricky part will be to estimate the percentage of the SAM that you think you can expect to capture. Try to avoid pure guesswork and do apply some intelligence to your analysis (the business slang word is "guestimate").

The big question is this: Can the expected market share justify the investment? (More about financial evaluation methodologies is found in chapter 9, "Financial Modeling and Evaluation.")

4. **Is the needed ecosystem ready for your innovation?** Let's say you invented the telephone. Your invention will not become pervasive until the infrastructure will be ready with a web of connections that will be able to route calls from person A to person B.

5. **What will the cost of the product be?** Will people pay the price you need to charge so this venture is profitable? Just look at personal computers. The first modern-era computer was built in the 1940s, yet it took another forty to fifty years before it became affordable as a household item. (As I discuss later, it had its use in government and high-end commercial applications.)

6. **Is there any alternative solution that will compete against your product?** Even if you are the only airline to fly from city A to city B, it doesn't mean you have cornered the market. Your competition includes trains, buses, shuttle services, car rentals, ships, and perhaps even videoconferencing (in lieu of a face-to-face meeting).

7. **What is your business model?** How will people acquire your product? Will it be an off-the-shelf purchase by the end customer (selling cartons of eggs in the supermarket)? Or will you sell it to other businesses to be integrated into

their product higher in the food chain (selling eggs to bakeries)? What are the distribution channels? What is your marketing strategy? Will you provide training for salespeople?

8. **What is the timeline to actualize the idea?** Will it still be relevant when the product is ready to launch in the marketplace? What are the odds that by that time more competitors will have entered the market as well?

9. **What is your barrier of entry?** How easy is it to copycat your idea, product, or service? One thing to remember: Having a patent is not a protection unless you have millions of dollars set aside to sue any infringements.

10. **Have you budgeted adequate internal resources to fund the product development?** Or do you need external funding? A development budget must include all the phases to product commercialization, as this very list demonstrates.

11. **Is the product scalable?** Is it relevant to other geographies or market segments as is, or do you need to modify it to fit other markets? What is your high-volume manufacturing strategy? Will you build it yourself or subcontract to a third-party manufacturing house?

12. **What is your quality assurance plan?** How will you make sure your product will work reliably in the summer in Saudi Arabia as well as in the winter in Finland? What is the product's resistance to vibrations? (Can it absorb a fall on the floor every now and then?) What about its water resistance? (Will it survive a rainy day or your sweat while working out with it?) Its electromagnetic

field interference? (Remember the days in the early 1980s when your notebook computer would freeze when you boarded an airplane?) Has it any health side effects? And the list goes on and on. In the case of a software product, test it beyond its limits. If you expect 1,000 hits per hour to a website or an application, test it with 100 times that much to make sure it won't crash in the event of overwhelming demand.

13. **Does your product include any controlled substances and therefore must be certified by a standards organization?** Does it need to be permitted by any government agency? Does it need to be approved by insurance agencies?

14. **What is your customer support plan?** Will you develop and train staff for a toll-free help line? Will you establish repair labs and train technicians to perform the work?

15. **Do you intend to offer warranty plans?** Remember, warranty plans are not created just to satisfy a product checklist. They are written to guarantee that the quality of the product is good enough so that product returns will not bankrupt you, nor will they create a bad reputation for your brand.

16. **Do you need to develop documentation (a user manual, technical specs, etc.) to go along with the product?** If you target the global market, you need to plan for multilingual documentation (i.e., budget for the translation work).

Some of your initial answers to these checklist questions may be no, yet don't rush to kill the initiative. It is very likely that some of the obstacles have solutions that will turn the answer into a yes. Some of the workaround may be a new business model that will make it more feasible.

Use the Checklist to Draft a Business Plan

Once you decide to adopt a new idea, you should create a business plan that dives into the details surrounding it. A business plan is a written document that describes what the goals of the new business are and how it is going to achieve these goals. At the highest level, the business plan must define the motivation for the new idea, its feasibility, its economics (financial justification), the implementation plan (schedule and budget), as well as its risks and mitigations. Each item in the checklist of questions for which you have a positive answer will become the first draft of your business plan.

Permit me a brief aside at this juncture. Business innovation has its reward by allegedly creating some kind of competitive advantage, but it also has the risks inherent in trying something new and unknown. The risk in disruptive innovation is in the difficulty to predict its market acceptance. The risks in process changes can be addressed by planning the appropriate risk mitigations. The risks in incremental product and service features can be easily mitigated by allowing them to be optional at first. Whatever the risk is, a good business plan must include risk mitigation measures. (For more about risk see chapter 17, "Risk Management for New Products.")

Creating an entire detailed business plan costs time and money; thus, the value of the checklist is to serve as a quick go/no-go gate before you invest in planning the details. With each version of the business plan you write, you may uncover new obstacles, and these must be addressed before you move forward. This is a chicken and an egg question. In this case, "laying the egg" is not a one-time event. You lay the egg in phases. (This is not a biological statement, however.) You don't need to answer all the questions on day one, but rather develop a feasibility study plan that will take you through several go/no-go gates, each to answer some of the questions before you move on to research additional questions.

Some of the questions are statistical in nature; thus the first phase may be a small sample, the next gate will be a larger sample, and so on. Large corporations have people on the payroll to go through the innovation process. The individuals are getting paid to do it, while for the corporation it is a tiny fraction of their budget. In case of entrepreneurship, however, life is more complicated.

A potential entrepreneur will start the process while still working for a previous employer. Only when convinced that he passed enough gates will he quit the job and start spending more time on his new idea. If the entrepreneur is already out of a job, she wants to move through these feasibility gates rather quickly because she needs to raise some money to start collecting a paycheck to put some food on the table. Obviously, when the entrepreneur is independently wealthy the time pressure is less tactical but more strategic: This individual still wants to launch the new idea as early as possible and get some return on the time and money invested in the venture.

Okay. Let's turn back to the six categories I identified at the beginning of the chapter as essential ones for you to consider in your new product or service evaluation process. Bear with me, here, because it may feel like I'm being redundant by presenting categories that were touched on in the checklist. That's true to some extent, but in my experience, you can't know enough about each of these core elements of the business plan, particularly at this stage in the process.

Company's Strategy

First and foremost, any new product must fit the company's strategy.[3] If the company's strategy is to double its market share in Russia, for example, new products that address the needs of the Russian market will get priority.

In one of my tenures within the corporate world, our business unit had a high concentration of three customers that accounted for approximately 70 percent of the revenue. This was a risky situation because any hiccup in one customer's business could have rattled our business results too much. In order to extricate ourselves from this risky situation, one of our strategic goals was to add two more customers to the other three revenue generators, and after three years, we accomplished that goal. This came with a price, as we had to turn down good business opportunities that did not contribute to this strategic goal of adding new major customers to the top list. The reward, however, was risk reduction through having five major customers rather than the three we had before.

In the world of start-ups, company strategy is generally pretty simple and straightforward. Strategic fit is addressed during the search for funding sources. The start-up founder(s) must look for VC firms whose investment strategy fits the start-up's vision or invention. If the start-up falls outside of a VC firm's investment boundaries, that firm will simply not even consider the opportunity. I have hundreds of VC firms and investors in my Rolodex. When I'm working on a fund-raising project, my first step is to find the relevant VC firms with an applicable investment strategy. This process takes many hours and normally yields a subset of around 10 to 20 percent who are candidates I put on the short list to be contacted. The second step in this search process is to review these VC firms' portfolios to make sure none of them have invested in one of my client's competitors. (If they did, they must be erased from the short list.) This is a long and tedious two-step process, which normally requires that some form of retainer be paid to the outside consultant to justify the overhead time invested in preparing for the process.

R&D Budget Considerations

As you'll see with manufacturing considerations later in the chapter, the R&D budget issues are also threefold. They are limitations, capabilities, and start-ups.

1. **Limitations.** Even a large company doesn't have unlimited resources. Large companies are normally organized according to business units, and each one is allocated its own limited R&D budget. This usually allows for only a few new products per year per business unit, the selection process having revealed which ones to pursue and which ones to drop.[4] (Please refer to the checklist previously mentioned for subjects that should be included in the selection process.)

2. **Capabilities.** Another concern is the capabilities represented by the R&D team(s) within a large company. If the entire R&D team consists of nothing but chemical engineers, for instance, and the new product requires a software component, the obvious disconnect needs to be addressed, either by hiring a software team or partnering with an outside software development provider.

3. **Start-ups.** In a large company, the R&D effort is performed by a small percentage of the entire team. The opposite is the case with start-ups. The largest percentage of the company's expenses goes to pay for R&D activities. Therefore, the founder(s) needs to pay careful consideration to hiring the right R&D personnel. Taking the previous example, the ideal situation is for the start-up to find one person who can handle both the chemical engineering part and the software part. Otherwise, the small start-up would have to hire two people, which doubles the cost. Later in the start-up's life, it will have both a chemical engineering team and a software team, but at the early stage, it needs to minimize the payroll drain. A multitalented person is a big asset.

Manufacturing and Supply Chain Considerations

Manufacturing's main issues are threefold: technology, capacity and cost.[5] You can ask a series of questions about each issue to get a better handle on how these issues relate to and complement one another.

1. **Technology:** Do you have the technology to build it in-house? Or hire a subcontractor? Or develop the technology in house? The devil is in the details again. You need to look into the technology specifications to answer this question correctly. You may have a plastic molding factory, but does its precision capabilities meet the requirement of the new product? Or can it handle the specific type of plastic you need? Do you need to invest in additional technology? If so, it must be accounted for when you perform the ROI analysis for the project.

2. **Capacity:** Do you have the capacity to build the predicted number of units (along with all the other products this particular facility is already committed to making)? When evaluating capacity, you need to take into account a certain level of rejects, which could be high during the initial batches of a new product. Also ask yourself whether you need to invest in additional production capacity. If so, it needs to be accounted for when you perform the ROI analysis for the project.

3. **Cost:** Can the product be built at a profitable cost for the market target price? The emphasis here is to start with market target price and reverse engineer to calculate the product cost. How much will the early runs cost? What is the expected cost reduction (learning curve) over time? (More about it in the learning curve discussion)

In addition to looking at these three manufacturing issues, review the supply chain needs. Ask questions such as these: Can we trust all the sources? Do we agree to be associated with them, or should we find alternative sources? A small business can do whatever it wants; large corporations, on the other hand, pay attention to their corporate image as it is being reflected via its business partners and supply chain sources.

All of this is true for a start-up with these important differences:

- In the case of manufacturing, a subcontractor usually handles that function.

- In the case of a non-software start-up, the cost of early prototypes has a significant impact on the overall budget, and the initial built quantities must be carefully considered.

- In the case of 3-D physical products, the most economical technology to use in making the first few samples is likely to be a 3-D printer.

- In the case of a digital electronics product, a field-programmable gate array (FPGA) is likely to be the most economical technology for early prototypes.

- In the case of a new chemical or food product, your initial mixing can be done manually in your garage or kitchen; or rent time in a lab if you need more sophisticated equipment.

Go-to-Market Channels

The channel to the market is another critical element in the food chain. (I discuss channel strategies at length in chapter 11, "Business Development," and in chapter 13, "Sales.") For the purpose of this section, you need only to understand whether you have the needed go-to-market channel relationships. Or do you need to develop such relationships alongside the R&D progress? Having access to a channel is not enough; it must be the right channel for the specific product and market segment you target.[6]

Say you are in the building material business, for example, and you sell your mature products strictly in retail stores to small general contractors and do-it-yourself hobbyists. Now, however, you want to introduce a new product to big construction firms. Consequently, the channel to these potential big customers is likely to be different. You probably will need to hire new salespeople who have established relationships with those firms, or you will have to outsource the sales function to a distributor that specializes in this market segment.

Once again, the situation is different for a start-up. Initial market feedback is critical to its survival. Therefore, interacting with customers falls initially to the founder(s). These relationships must be maintained because the same customers that give the initial feedback are likely to turn into the first actual paying customers once the product is out. In cases where the original founder fails to cement these customer relationships and connections, he or she must add a cofounder with these proper relationships early on in the start-up's life. Some start-ups make the fatal mistake of developing the product first and worrying about how to market and sell it later. In most such cases, the end result is a great engineering breakthrough that no one wants to buy.

Once the start-up is mature enough to reach out to additional customers, it needs to hire more business development people (usually part-time) with the right skills and market connections.

Organization

Different companies have different organizational philosophies and strategies based on the type of markets they serve, the diversity of their product lines, their overall geographical deployments, and the company's unique culture. In medium-size companies, all the departments' managers report to the CEO, with a VP responsible for each department. Very large corporations often have multiple considerations and more often than not end up with some convoluted structure because it is practically impossible to come up with a perfectly ideal organizational solution. Each situation is different, and there is no right or wrong approach to organizational structure that fits all situations. It just needs to be in sync with the company's overall strategy for growth. (In chapter 15, "The Human Factor—the Organization," I review a variety of organizational structures.) For the purpose of evaluating new product or service ideas, the main question to answer is whether the new project fits in the existing organization structure. And if so, how? Or does it require some organizational change?

Finance

The simplified financial evaluation process is summarized in three words: return on investment (ROI). As usual, though, the complexity is in the details. This section will just touch on some of the ideas an evaluative financial checklist should contain. (Much more elaborate coverate of the financial considerations regarding innovation is found in chapter 9, "Financial Modeling and Evaluation.")

I cover the source for the "R" (Return) in ROI later in this section, where I discuss how to present the revenue numbers for the purpose of a robust financial evaluation.

Let's first touch on the "I" (Investment) of ROI.

The "Investment" in ROI

Your consideration of "investment" must include all functions related to the new product. Obviously, R&D is one such function, which is the first major phase in the implementation of the project. Many make the mistake of considering only R&D when looking at the investment required. It is critical to consider all the other functions as well in calculating the ROI.

Remember to report whether or not the project will need to hire additional resources. I've seen many cases where the project was approved but, later on, securing permission to hire more personnel got bogged down in some other bureaucratic approval path. Come to the new product review meeting with the hiring requisitions to be signed on the spot. (A trick I learned the hard way over years of service in the corporate world.)

Here are some of the non-R&D investments that must be thrown into the ROI analysis.

Technology: Does the new product use a variation of the same technology platform as your other products? Or does it require some basic technology investment?

Manufacturing: Does the new product require new manufacturing tooling (whether in-house or by a subcontractor)?

Intellectual Property: Filing patents is an obvious investment of time and money, but you also need to budget for legal fees to protect the intellectual property over the years.

Marketing: The investment in launching and selling a new product is extensive, involving competition analysis, product documentation, sales force training, customer training, public relations, launch events, monitoring social media, search engine optimizations (SEOs), free samples, discounted early sales, warranty expenses, and so on. If the product is in a totally different industry, you'll need to budget for sending company attendees to additional industry events and paying for other organizational memberships.

Sales: Do you have the right sales people with the proper connections? If not, new ones must be hired. The pay structure for salespeople has a significant commission component to it. This creates some resistance among salesmen and women to support new products because it requires more effort on their part (educating their customers versus just using the easy ongoing purchase orders pipeline), and it reduces their commission potential because initial purchases are normally smaller in volume.

All of the non-R&D investments outlined above must be included in the investment side of the ROI formula.

The "Return" in ROI

Modeling the "return" is not a simple task either. The main number in the formula—the top-line revenue—is based on an estimate, and so it must be treated as such. (Different techniques on how to produce this revenue estimate are explained in chapter 5, "Estimating Demand for a New Product.")

A tricky disconnect can result from the uncertainty in the baseline assumptions. In order to estimate the ROI for financial modeling purposes, the ("most likely") top line number is often multiplied by a confidence level, which results in a lower top line number. Another technique to deal with the revenue uncertainty is to run several scenarios in the model: most likely, best-case and worst-case. The purpose of the best-case scenario is to assess production capacity readiness should the introduction be overly successful. The purpose of the worst-case scenario is to evaluate if the ROI is still positive under these conditions. If the worst-case scenario shows a negative ROI, it doesn't necessarily mean you should kill the project. Often, additional mitigation measures may solve the issue and turn the ROI to a positive.

During the implementation phase, one "party line" scenario must be used to avoid confusion and to assure that the entire organization is working off the same set of assumptions. It is okay to use the worst-case scenario to evaluate ROI sensitivities, but it is not okay to plan the production based on that worst case because you risk not having enough products to serve market demand.

The second tricky part is the learning curve effect. Make sure you take into account the production cost as a function of time. The first batches are likely to cost more, but be careful not to kill the project because of it (only to budget for it). What's important is the long-term volume cost, not the higher initial cost.

The third complicated part is modeling the cost and revenue per unit as a function of time. Sometimes, the variations are not the same. If you choose to take inflation into account, the common practice is to use the same percentage of inflation for both product cost and product price. In some situations, however, the deviations are different. For example, there is a given price range that people pay for airplane tickets; fuel prices fluctuate, however, and may rise beyond what the customers will be willing to absorb.

The fourth complexity is in the time difference between the manufacturing cost and the sales revenue. Large corporations with deep enough pockets and sufficient credit lines simply decide the accounting methodology based either on when a product cost is recognized (i.e., when the product manufacture happens or when the product is sold) or on when the product revenue is recognized (when the product is shipped or when the invoice was issued/the customer paid). They don't care much about these issues; they just need to be consistent in their accounting procedures. For a smaller company, though, this cash flow time gap could make or break its survival, and it must be taken into account in the financial modeling. This is especially critical when the subject is new products. In a very steep ramping up of a new product, the production costs are likely to be incurred several months before the revenue from sales flows in. This puts a significant strain on the cash flow of the young company and must be planned for so you won't find yourself with empty pockets prematurely.

Once the financial model is developed, there is one major execution difference between large companies and start-ups. In a large company, the financial optimization is normally done for the entire life cycle, from inception to market maturity to the end of life phase out.

Start-ups, by contrast, are usually funded in tranches: Each round of funding is just enough to execute to the next milestone. If it runs out of money before it achieves the next milestone, the start-up is dead, or severely penalized (while, in a large company, you will just get a slap on the hand). This requires careful planning to attain each milestone in minimum time and with minimum resources so the start-up's founder(s) can justify why investors should continue to invest.

Okay. Your team has preliminarily evaluated an idea or two using the New Idea Evaluation Checklist. And you've decided what type of business innovation best suits each idea. Now it's time to estimate new product demand, which is a mandatory step in evaluating the economics of the new idea and is the subject of our next chapter.

Takeaways

- The devil is in the details.

- Developing a new product or service is a multidisciplinary process. All organizational functions must participate in it.

- Refer to the New Idea Evaluation Checklist and the Checklist Summary Chart when evaluating innovation ideas.

CHAPTER 5

ESTIMATING DEMAND FOR A NEW PRODUCT

Estimating the demand for a new product or service is a crucial step in any new product's business plan.[1] You must also learn how to use the estimated demand in your financial model for the project. The demand estimation serves two purposes. Before the project starts, it is used as a measuring tool to evaluate the economics of the project. This is a living document, to be updated periodically. After the project reaches the commercialization phase, the demand estimation document can be used as a sales forecast and supply chain planning tool, but once again, treat it as a living document and update it periodically.

Before we take a look at estimating demand for specific types of products, a quick word about terminology. Though they have subtle nuances, I use the words "forecast," "estimation," and "projection" interchangeably throughout this chapter. And please note that all the estimation and forecasting techniques discussed in this chapter are relevant to all types of new products.

Forecasting Demand for Evolutionary Products

Evolutionary products are easier to forecast than brand-new products. If the new product is just a newly evolved flavor within an existing product category, your sales history is pretty well known. All you have to do is estimate the phase over from the older generation to the new one. If it is a new market entry with an existing product, estimate the market share you are going to capture over time based on your experience from the previous segments and the competitive situation in the new one.

When you're looking at consumer products that are continually evolving, two methods have proven to be valuable in estimating market share: focus groups and select trial markets. In general, marketing people sometimes cycle through several rounds of each method, with a bigger sample each time. And an important factor to take into account in your estimation is brand strength. If the new product is launched by a strong brand name, its adoption rate will be faster compared to a product that is launched by a new entry start-up supplier.

Focus Groups

Focus groups involve having a random sample of consumers try the new product and answer questions related to the likelihood of their buying it, either on a trial basis or long term as their preferred choice in the future. The focus groups need to be designed in a way that will include participants who represent all the market segments the product is targeted toward, at the correct proportions that represent the different segments of the target market.

An early-stage start-up with a tight budget should start the market research with a small focus group of friends and family and expand later to a larger group once they get the funding to do so. Take the preliminary results from that initial focus group to investors that will inject additional capital to fund a more comprehensive testing of the market.

This methodology is similar to research conducted among other risky projects. Oil and gas exploration is a perfect example. The geological studies of a new exploration area are done in phases. You invest a little for a preliminary study. If the results pass a certain threshold, you invest additional funds in a more in-depth study. Perhaps a few more cycles will be needed. After you have gained enough confidence, you perform a trial drill in the area. Perhaps a few test drills will be required if you are not sure about the exact location of the oil or natural gas reserves. Only if the trial drill shows positive economic results should you consider starting production drilling in more locations in the same area or just converting the test dig into a production well.

Select Trial Markets

The second method to use after completing a series of focus groups is to launch the new product on a limited basis in a few selected trial markets. The trial market ideally aims to duplicate the entire marketing mix—promotion and distribution as well as product—on a smaller scale before the company commits significant resources to a full launch campaign. This methodology replicates, typically in one or a very few areas, what is planned for a national launch. Therefore, the results are carefully monitored so that any lessons learned can be extrapolated to project national results and strategy adjustments that need to be made.

The downsides of such market trials need to be understood, though. These include the following:

1. A small trial market may not be a good representation of the entire market.

2. Testing your products among trial markets runs the risk of sending warning signals to your competitors.

3. The costs involved in selecting and hosting trial market tests can be expensive.

4. The time it takes to design and implement this method can be prohibitive.

Estimating Demand for Products with No Sales History

A bigger challenge by far is estimating the future revenue and profits of a new product category with no sales history data to extrapolate from. The trade-off in forecasting is between the time and the cost of the forecast. The higher the confidence level you seek, the longer it will take and the higher the cost of the study will be. One caveat to keep in mind: If you wait to have 100 percent confidence in your estimate, it is too late to act on the information. Another reason not to spend too much time on product studies is the possibility that one of your rivals will introduce a competitive product and you may lose the opportunity to be first to the market. You'll find much more about these trade-offs in the *Harvard Business Review* article "How to Choose the Right Forecasting Technique"[2] and *Research for Marketing Decisions.*[3]

Don't Overdo Market Research— Focus Group or Trial Market Wise

In the mid-1950s, Ford realized the socioeconomic shift in America, with many baby boomers' families entering the middle class. It decided to design the perfect middle class vehicle for them. The company performed extensive market research in the planning and design of the new Edsel vehicle. The details of its styling and specifications were the result of a sophisticated market analysis and R&D effort that was supposed to guarantee its broad acceptance by the buying public.[4]

Ford invested $250 million in the project, but the company ended up losing $350 million! The company predicted first year's sales to be 200,000 vehicles but sold 68,000—about a third of what they had estimated.

Despite Ford's extensive market studies, the Edsel's launch was a failure. What happened? One of the reasons was that by the time the new model was introduced, the market preferences had shifted, and consumers had become more price sensitive due to the 1957 recession. The moral of the story: If you wait until you have 100 percent of the information to make a decision, it's already too late.

Sometimes a new product may snatch customers from multiple segments. For example, the flavored water market grossed more than $20 billion in 2015, with compound annual growth (CAGR) of 11 percent.[5] The industry is successful because it captured customers both from the soda drinkers segment as well as the more health conscious previous water drinkers; in addition, some of the suppliers designed appealing bottles to entice emotional buyers who were attracted to the product based on its aesthetic appeal. When you estimate demand for a new product, make sure to analyze what contribution adjacent market segments may provide.

Estimating Demand for Emotional Products

Estimating the demand for emotional products is trickier. An emotional product is a product that satisfies an emotional need. (This subject is so important it warrants its own chapter in part VI.) If, back in April 1975, you had asked Gary Dahl how many pet rocks he was expecting to sell, he would have said he didn't have a clue. (The full story behind the pet rock's overnight success is found in chapter 19, "Emotional Products.")

For lower-cost products, it is relatively inexpensive to build few prototypes and use focus groups to assess their reaction to the product appeal and price elasticity. If the product requires a significant investment, however—such as in shooting a new movie—the focus group method is not practical.

In the case of a new movie, a "comp" (short for comparable) methodology is used.[6] You are looking at other products out in the market and how much people paid to produce them. In the movie business, the comps are derived from three main types of historical data:

1. Similar movies in the same genre (comedies, drama, horror, etc.)

2. Cast/celebrity appeal (Which actors are playing the lead roles?)

3. Distribution contracts (It is common in the entertainment industry to presell a project to a distributor, which often will prepay the distribution rights, thus removing some of the risks in regards to the market acceptance.)

This comp methodology is also commonly used in real estate. When you try to sell a property, commercial or residential, you look at recent transactions in the same vicinity and come up with a price per square foot based on similar properties in that neighborhood. Once you have the estimated price per square foot, you multiply it by the square footage of the property being listed for sale; that is pretty much the best estimate you can have. Later, you may increase or reduce that price depending on the condition of the property and recent additional improvements that were made.

Estimating Demand for B2B Products

When dealing with B2B customers, the process changes somewhat. The number of potential customers for your products drops dramatically, yet the buying potential of each one is huge; thus, the cost of a mistake enormous.

Let's ignore for a moment the competitive environment. The fact that we are now dealing with very few customers doesn't require lots of statistical market studies and focus groups. It does, however, require good relationships with the major players of the targeted market segment so they will accept your request to meet and pick their brains. You don't need any statistical sample. You basically can interview 100 percent of the market for feedback. Thus, the demand estimation process becomes quite simple: The customer will tell you that if you do XYZ, they will buy so many units of the product from you. All you need to do is make XYZ happen. *Very simple.* When the two parties in the B2B equation are large corporations with practically no significant resource limitations, the process from here on is very straightforward: Just do it.

When the supplier is a small start-up, simplicity is not a word that leaps to mind. Even if you know how best to do XYZ, you don't have all the resources and funding to make it happen. This is the perfect example of "lay an egg and make chicken soup." Once you have an understanding with the customer about their need for an XYZ product, and their intent to work with you on that, but you don't yet have the funding to implement it, you have to use this customer intent as an argument to convince investors to fund the project. (We will cover fund-raising options in more detail in chapter 10, "Funding for a New Product or Service.")

For the purpose of estimating demand, the assumption here is that these few customers you talk to know their markets and should be able to give you some fairly reliable forecast of future XYZ sales.

Allow me to share with you a B2B customers example from my own work history.

A Leading Game Supplier and Motorola

When I ran a Digital Signal Processor (DSP) business unit for Motorola Semiconductors (later spun out as Freescale), we were hired by a leading Japanese game console supplier to provide the audio electronics for the game console they were making at that time. My immediate reward: I became my kids' hero overnight. The customer liked our technology; they viewed it as the one best suited to process audio signals in the game console. But there was a problem: None of the product configurations we offered were a perfect match for their needs. They required that we design a different product based on the same DSP platform. Estimating the revenue potential to justify the project became a simple matter of plugging the numbers into the equation. The customer knew exactly how many units they sold. They knew the growth rate. They also knew, based on history, the changeover pattern between a previous generation and a new generation of the product. All we needed to do was to plug their numbers into our planning spreadsheet. Their sales alone were so enormous that they justified the entire project and no further market analysis was required.

Forecasting Methods to Choose From

As I mentioned in the beginning of this chapter, estimating and forecasting are similar terms and are often used interchangeably. "Estimating," however, is usually used for long-term planning, even before the project starts, while "forecasting" is mainly used for the shorter term, such as next quarter or next year. Maybe because we are dealing here with new products, "estimate" is the more appropriate term to use.

Take a look at the descriptions of the methods that follow, each with its pros and cons.

Top-Down Estimate

When the total available market (TAM) is pretty predictable, try to research the history of similar product launches, and use that data as your guideline. If you launch a new type of cereal, obtain historical numbers of similar new cereal products, and use that historical penetration rate as your basic starting point. If you want to be conservative, use the worst example from all the historical cases, or even slightly less than the worst example. There is a risk in being too conservative, however. The conservative scenario may be so bad that it will kill the idea that otherwise could have been a successful product. You need to prepare the appropriate production capacity, but if the supply planning is too low, you may not be able to react to the higher market demand fast enough. The result? It could kill customers' interest in the product.

Segmented Top-Down Forecast

This method is similar to top-down forecasting, it's just applied separately to different market segments. This is more relevant to do in two particular cases: if the market reaction is expected to differ among different segments (e.g., a new electronic gadget may appeal to different groups based on how old they are or what they're able to afford) and if you plan to stage the launch to different segments at different times.

Bottom-Up Forecast

In the bottom-up forecast method, you ask each customer to give you their sales forecast and then you combine those to create yours. Very often, a B2B supplier will have a manageable number of top (potential) customers. Be advised, though, that any given customer's estimate is not a guarantee; at the end of the day, it is still an estimate. (Even if it is an existing customer, when it comes to a new product, there is no guarantee that they will buy it from you or at what quantities.) Nevertheless, the implied assumption here is that the customers will do a better job of estimating future sales because they are closer to the end users.

This methodology is doable if you have a limited number of potential customers, usually in a B2B situation. In case you are not sure about the level of commitments of these customers to your new product, you should multiply the estimates from each customer by your confidence level (probability) that this particular customer will indeed materialize.

Statistical Bottom-Up Forecast

If you are selling directly to end consumers, or if you have too many small-business customers, it is not practical to call all of them one by one. In this case, you go through the bottom-up process only with a sample of the market. You need to plan the sample(s) based on market segments and build your forecast based on the bottom-up results from each sample. (This is a variation on the "select trial markets" mentioned earlier as a method of forecasting demand for evolutionary products.)

In reality, people use several techniques to gain confidence in their ability to forecast/estimate product demand. If you are reluctant to trust your business's future based on one single methodology, it will be more reliable to choose from among several estimation strategies and get a range of forecasts, thus increasing your confidence level in the process.

Bass Diffusion Model

Estimating the market potential is not always enough. You may want to predict the adoption pattern as well, which normally could take several years. Here is where the Bass Diffusion Model comes to the rescue. Marketing research and science academic Frank M. Bass developed this model in 1969.[7] It consists of a simple mathematical equation that describes the process of how new products get adopted by first-time buyers in a population. The model presents a rationale of how current adopters and potential adopters of a new product interact. The basic principle of the model is that adopters can be classified as innovators (i.e., early adopters) or as imitators, and the speed and timing of adoption depends on their degree of innovativeness and the degree of imitation among adopters.

$$S(t) = m \ \frac{(p+q)^2}{p} \ \frac{e^{-(p+q)t}}{(1 + \frac{q}{p} e^{-(p+q)t})^2}$$

Where:

$S(t)$ is the rate of change of installed base (i.e., adoption).

m is the market potential.

p is the coefficient of innovation. The average value of has been found to be 0.03 and is often less than 0.01.

q is the coefficient of imitation. The average value of has been found to be 0.38, with a typical range between 0.3 and 0.5.

The Bass Diffusion Model can be applied only if there are some initial adoption data or by analyzing analogous products from the past.

This model has been widely influential in marketing and management science. In 2004, *Management Science* ranked it number five in its list of the ten most frequently cited papers in the fifty-year history of the journal, and it was the only marketing paper in the list. (The Bass Diffusion Model paper was reprinted in the journal's December 2004 issue.)

Takeaways

- Estimating the demand for a new product is a crucial step in the business plan, but it's hard to do when you're entering unknown territory with no sales history.

- Evolutionary products within an existing market or product category are pretty well-known. All you have to do is extrapolate from your older products and maybe also estimate the market share gain (if any) that is expected.

- In order to increase your confidence in estimating demand, use several forecasting methodologies to create a range of possible expected sales.

- The Bass Diffusion Model is a pretty good mathematical model, but the parameters for the formula can only be determined from actual initial sales or by looking at historical data of similar products.

PART III

HATCH THE CHICK
AND FOSTER ITS GROWTH

"A single arrow is easily broken, but not ten in a bundle."

—Japanese Proverb

CHAPTER 6

COMPETITION: IN BUSINESS, DIFFERENT IS OFTEN BETTER THAN BETTER

Very often when I am hired to help with a new product launch or fund-raising for a start-up, the client's presentation material is lacking any reference to competition. When I question them about it, the typical answer is some variation of "We are so much better, we don't have any competition." Wrong answer. There is no such thing as no competition. *Any* solution that addresses the same need is a potential competitor. Just ask yourself, how did the world survive before you invented this new product or service? Take another look at question #5 in the New Idea Evaluation Checklist in chapter 4 to remind yourself that competitors are lurking in every corner of the marketplace.

Because you will go up against competitors in the marketplace you should concentrate on what sets your new product or service apart. In this chapter, I describe ways in which you can showcase the uniqueness of your ideas. I also talk about the concept of "orthogonal differentiation," a term I coined during my tenure with Motorola.

Ways to Differentiate Your Product

Business competition appears under two major categories: linear and orthogonal competition. *Linear competition* is when a competitor offers a similar product but at a significantly lower cost and/or with a few extra features or with better performance. *Orthogonal competition* is when a competitor's products differentiate so much from others' that the business it creates is a whole different category for itself. Between these two extremes in real life, there is a continuum of degrees.

Simplify the Process to Achieve Significant Cost Differentiation

Many consider the Walt Disney Company (NYSE:DIS) to be the benchmark producer of animated feature films.[1] Its early classics were never big ROI successes, however—at least not initially. One of the reasons might have been the high cost of the 3-D near-reality animation style that Disney used in the 1940s and 50s. In those days, all the frames had to be created by hand, which meant that the production budget for each film was significant. In fact, costs often ran over the original estimates.

For example, Disney's *Cinderella* was a box office success when it premiered in 1950, grossing more than $4 million in initial distribution rentals, but production costs were a hefty

$2.2 million. It's little wonder that Disney's start-up experienced financial struggles in its early years. (To date, the lifetime revenue generated from *Cinderella* exceeds $250 million, however.)

An alternative approach was "limited animation." As the name implies, limited animation creates an image with abstract art, symbolism, and fewer drawings to create the same effect as in detailed hand-drawn 3-D animated films but at a much lower cost in terms of time, money, and labor.

In contrast to Disney's *Cinderella*, United Production of America's *Gerald McBoing Boing* was a limited animation film with a production budget of only $35,000. The lower budget reflected both the lower cost of the simplified technique as well as a different strategy in regard to the distribution approach. Instead of a full-length film targeted for the movie theaters, these short limited animation films were targeted for TV. Surprisingly, despite their simplified graphics (or maybe because of their simplicity), these films became extremely popular among children, and the Saturday morning cartoon shows quickly became household names. More recent examples of near-reality cartoons are *Frozen* (2013) and *Ferdinand* (2017). A recent example of limited animation is *The Simpsons* (started in 1989) and *Danger & Eggs* (2017).

Leverage the Power of Emotional Differentiation

Another way to differentiate your product or service in the marketplace is to tap into its power to evoke emotions. I can think of no better example to share in *Lay an Egg and Make a Chicken Soup* than that of free-range eggs. Although nothing could seem more benign, cage-free eggs have been a major cause for debate since the early days of the twenty-first century.[2]

The main motivation behind the cage-free promoters is animal welfare. But the shift from caged to cage-free is concerning for egg industry groups because they believe it will cause the price of eggs to increase to the point that consumers cannot afford to buy them, thereby causing a decline in the egg industry overall. Animal welfare advocates argue that costs will not change as drastically as industry groups claim they will and that the price of eggs will remain almost the same because the issue of whether the hens are housed in coops or allowed to range free does not make a huge difference in the cost of an egg.

That assertion seems to fly in the face of the facts, however. Cage-free eggs cost about 50 percent more to produce. The additional cost is a result of multiple factors, such as less production due to uncontrolled lighting, higher labor cost to collect the eggs, lost eggs, and an increase in real estate per hen. Nevertheless, retailers are listening to public opinions and perceptions that cage-free eggs are healthier (this claim had not been proven as of the time of this writing). Many have set timelines for their transition to selling nothing but cage-free eggs. The UK is leading this trend: 2012 was the first year when cage-free eggs constituted 50 percent of total eggs sold, up from merely 14 percent in 1995.[3]

This is yet another example illustrating that consumers are willing to pay a premium for an emotional product—driven, in this case, mainly by their concern for the hens' welfare. (For much more about emotional products, read chapter 19.) The differentiation here is not so much about better product (the eggs), but rather about a totally different emotional level of response to the product.

Blue Ocean Strategy—Underscore Dissimilarities

The subtitle of W. Chan Kim and Renée Mauborgne's *Blue Ocean Strategy* says it all when it comes to differentiation: *How to Create Uncontested Market Space and Make the Competition Irrelevant.*[4] One of the authors' analytical tools is called the "strategy canvas," in which they list different attributes of a product or service on the X-axis and the score of each attribute on the Y-axis. (My concept, "orthogonal differentiation" is a similar one.)

The best differentiation is one that shows significant *dissimilarities* between you and the competition in as many attributes as possible. The idea here is to downplay each of your competitors' alleged strengths while emphasizing your differentiating attributes. If, for instance, your competitor promotes their product by labeling it "low cost," you call it "cheap" and "you get what you pay for." If your competitor promotes "performance," you negate it as "overengineered" and "minimal function at an inflated cost."

Another way to use the dissimilarities approach to design a new product or service is to map out your competitors' mix of features. Then, take the opposite of that mix of features to create a competitive product. Ideally, you want to imagine something as different as possible from the one you want to compete against. This is easier said than done, though, because at the same time, you must make sure that the blue-oceaned product you came up with is one that people will pay for.

Additional tools are presented in the book and on the Blue Ocean website (www.blueoceanstrategy.com).

Orthogonal Differentiation

While managing the marketing department for a $500 million business unit at Motorola, I coined a term and a concept called "orthogonal differentiation." In mathematics, orthogonal lines are at right angles to each other (90°). Orthogonal lines (or vectors) are totally independent of each other. One line cannot be described mathematically as a function of the other. (Other fields have borrowed the term, and it usually means irrelevant or independent.)

Orthogonal differentiation in marketing means distinguishing your product or service based on a totally independent attribute that is not used by your competitors.

Let's look at a few companies who have put this approach into practice.

HomePlate Peanut Butter

Peanut butter is probably one of the most commoditized product categories. Did you know there are more than seven hundred peanut butter suppliers in the world? In such a crowd, it is difficult to differentiate your variety from the others. Many try to be the cheapest. Some try to differentiate based on quality or organic ingredients. A few have chosen to move up the food chain (literally) by introducing food products that include peanut butter as one of the ingredients, such as peanut butter cookies, peanut butter–filled pretzels, and so on.

According to HomePlate Peanut Butter's cofounder and CEO Clint Greenleaf, the company took an orthogonal approach by focusing on one specific market segment: baseball players.[5] Peanut butter is as much a part of America's favorite pastime as hot dogs, sunflower seeds, and bubble gum. (Players gave up chewing tobacco in 2011.) It's a tasty tradition that stretches from dugout to dugout. HomePlate Peanut Butter was founded by a group of former professional baseball players who relied on peanut butter as a quick and inexpensive way to stay fueled and fit. By focusing on this market segment, HomePlate became the official peanut butter of the Professional Baseball Clubhouse Managers Association. They grew very quickly to be popular in other sports, and their products are available in thousands of stores all across the United States.

Chrysler Minivan

The station wagon used to be a popular vehicle worldwide because it was configured as a high-occupancy/large cargo space car to accommodate families. (The last row of seats could usually fold down to provide additional storage when needed.) The next size up was a full van, which was too big and too gas hungry for family use. A few Chrysler (NYSE:FCAU) engineers and product planners recognized that there was a gap between the station wagon and the full-size van, and they began to promote a concept within the company that was initially called a "garageable van." The garageable van had several false starts, which were initially shot down by company bureaucrats. Lee Iacocca finally gave the go-ahead to the concept in the early 1980s. None of the other U.S. car manufacturers had any vehicle like it.

The minivan was introduced in 1983 and became a hit almost overnight, with peak sales of roughly 500,000 vehicles per year for more than two decades thereafter. The Chrysler minivan started to taper off—down to about 200,000 vehicles

ORTHOGONAL DIFFERENTIATION
OF THE CHRYSLER MINIVAN

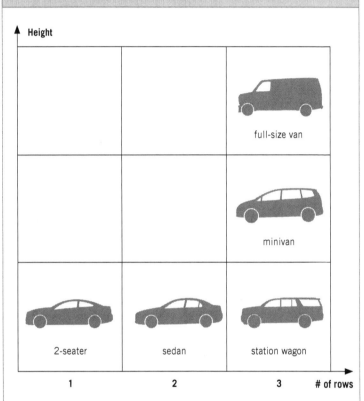

Filling an empty gap between the full-size van and the station wagon.

per year—only at the beginning of the twenty-first century. The reason for the decline was that other automakers had since introduced comparable models in the market along with the rising popularity of sport utility vehicles (SUVs).[6]

Orthogonal differentiation of the Chrysler minivan: filling an empty gap between the full-size van and the station wagon.

Make sure your innovation team members have lots of opportunities to discuss these and other ways to differentiate your products and services. It's a fun process that keeps you abreast of the competitors on the playing field and sparks imaginative ideas about how to beat them.

Takeaways

- The best way to overtake the competition is to change the rules of the game to a point where your competitor becomes irrelevant.

- Don't try to be better; be different.

- Can you set your product apart through a significant cost differentiation? With an emotional product? By underscoring an independent (orthogonal) attribute?

CHAPTER 7

BUSINESS MODEL

The term "business model" has been defined as an abstract representation of a business architecture of all interrelated products and/or services the organization offers and the financial arrangements linked to them.[1] (I simplified the original definition a little.)

The following paragraphs describe the two most commonly used types of business models—linear and platform—as well as such related complex platform models as the pharmaceutical based and the Internet based (as exemplified in Software as a Service (SaaS) and the PC open system).

Linear Business Model

In the old days, a chicken farmer would raise hens in the backyard and sell the mature ones directly to the consumer (most likely bartering them for some other goods). The consumer would slaughter the chicken, clean it, cook it, and eat it. A pretty simple transaction between the producer (the farmer) and the consumer (the diner). This unembellished exchange applied a linear business model.

As societies became more specialized, slaughterhouses and butcher shops emerged as middle entities between the chicken farmer and the consumers. Even with those extra players and steps, the linear business model was still being applied, in which a business takes in raw material, creates finished products or services by adding value to it, sells to a customer (usually for a profit), and the customer pays the business for the products or services acquired. As I described in the "Innovating for B2B Customers" section of chapter 3, when entity X sells to entity Y and both are businesses, it is called business-to-business (B2B). When entity X is a business and entity Y is the final consumer, it is called business-to-consumer (B2C). A linear business model is straightforward (no pun intended): You pay for what you buy. Nothing more, nothing less.

Platform Business Model

A platform business model is more complex and has limitless variations. There is no one-to-one linkage between the product or service and the revenue stream. Several attempts have been made in the literature to define the term "platform business model," but I don't particularly like any of them. Here is my shot at defining it: A platform business model is one that facilitates matrixed business transactions between multiple entities in the ecosystem where the money flow (often referred to as "monetization flow") doesn't necessarily correlate directly with the physical products or services flow.

Although the term was introduced at the start of the Internet revolution, variations on the platform business model existed long before the advent of the Internet.

What's the Difference Between Linear & Platform?

A simple example that illustrates how the linear differs from the platform business model is the amenity of public restrooms in different countries. In many cities around the globe, you pay a fee to use a public restroom. This is the linear business model. In the United States, restrooms for the public are usually free of charge, but you are expected to buy something at the same store or restaurant that made the restroom available. By buying something you indirectly pay for using the restroom the establishment maintains. This is the platform business model.

Another variation of applying the platform business model—this one from the mid-twentieth century—is Bannister Babies.[2]

Before people could afford their own cameras, and long before smart phones with cameras became a common commodity, people would go to a professional photographer's studio on special occasions to have their family photos taken. The photographer took the photos, developed the negative film, printed the pictures, and sold them to the subject of the prints.

Then, in the 1940s, along came Constance Bannister. She had studied photography during the 1930s and, over the years, became famous mostly for the baby photos she created. Her business model was particularly unorthodox for those days. Rather than charging the parents for the prints, she had them sign a release giving her ownership of the negatives. She then built her business around producing prints to be used for advertising, for publication in books, and even for a line of baby dolls based on her photos. Into the 1950s, Bannister Babies photographs were widely distributed and seen frequently. They appeared on television shows hosted by Perry Como, Frank Sinatra, and others. The name "Constance Bannister" became synonymous with babies, with Jack Parr bestowing upon her the title "World's Most Famous Baby Photographer."

Pharmaceutical Based Platform Model

A more complex example of a platform business model is the pharmaceutical (or pharma) industry. A pharma provider needs to sell at multiple levels. The model described here is for the U.S. market. Countries with socialized medicine might use a variation on the model.

First and foremost, the pharma provider needs to get its new product approved by the relevant government authority. Second, on the business development front, the health insurance companies need to add the new drug to their approved/covered list of medications. (In countries with socialized medicine, the health insurance providers are government agencies paid by tax money. It is not free, but only perceived to be. The business model is different.) The third front is to educate doctors about the new drug. It is common practice in the industry to get the doctors' attention by providing them with some perks—but not too many so as to avoid accusations of conflicts of interest or bribes. The fourth front is the network of pharmacies, and last but not least are the end users—the patients who will actually ingest, inhale, or inject the medicinal drug. In some countries, advertising a drug to end consumers is not allowed. In many other countries it is. I always get a chuckle when actors in the pharma ads on American TV ask the lay audience to tell their doctor about a given new medicine.

On the flip side of the pharma complex platform model, end consumers have to deal with multiple entities as well. First, they buy medical insurance (or obtain insurance provided by their employer or government). The purpose of the health insurance, like any other insurance, is to make health costs more constant, with fewer unexpected fluctuations. In most cases, the health insurance companies are staying profitable: That is, on average, their income from the premiums exceeds their payouts to cover patients' medical expenses. Second, when consumers need medical attention, they will go see a doctor. The doctor will get paid partially by the insurance, with the patient paying the balance (deductible). When the patients/consumers need medication, they will go to the pharmacy to get it; and, once again, a portion will be covered by insurance, while the consumer will pay the deductible. An added layer of complexity occurs in cases where the consumer cannot afford a certain treatment or medication and has to find a credit source to finance it.

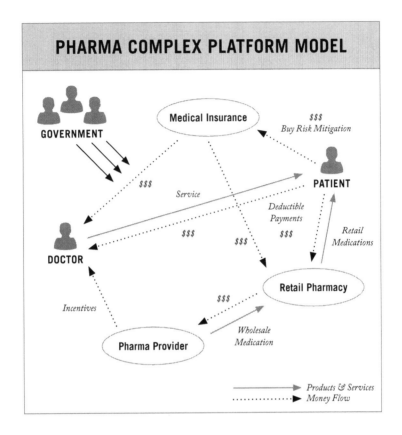

Internet-Based Platform Model

As I mentioned in the introduction to this section, the platform business model became more popular after the Internet became the way of life. Therefore, let's learn how to recognize it by looking at the following two variations of this complex platform business model.

Software as a Service Model

The software you use can reside inside your own personal computer or it can reside (often called "hosted") in some remote computer and send you the results of whatever operation you used it for. Three main business models are commonly used for software:

1. You purchase the software and pay a one-time fee for it.

2. You pay a monthly license fee to use the software (basically, in layman's terms, you rent the software).

3. Software as a Service, or SaaS, is a software distribution model in which the provider hosts application software in its data center (i.e., computer system) and makes it available to customers over the Internet for a fee. Consumers pay either on a flat-fee basis (such as a monthly subscription) or on a per-use basis (such as for each minute of use).

TrendKite uses the SaaS model. As the company's CEO, Erik Huddleston, explains it, TrendKite's platform harnesses big data and analytics to measure the impact that news coverage has on a brand's reputation, website traffic, and business goals. Here's how this works with TrendKite's public relations clients, for example.

Public relations (PR) campaigns command attention, engage audiences, and draw people to interact with your brand. TrendKite's PR measurement tools show how mentions of your business in the media influence and contribute to moving people down the marketing funnel. With TrendKite's technology, PR Attribution, it is possible to measure the total number of people who visit your website after reading a given media article—regardless of there being a link to your website in the article or not. TrendKite does this for more than *4 million* global publications. This is obviously a complicated algorithm that links an individual's reading an article about your company to his or her later visit(s) to your website, even when the two actions were not immediately linked to each other.

Let's look at the application of the SaaS model in a different context to show its advantages in the area of cash flow.

Equipment rent or lease models may create a cash flow gap because the supplier invests capital in acquiring the asset up front but monetizes its value over a long period of time. Obviously, the asset lessor has the option to finance the purchase, in which case it just needs to make sure that the average expected income from the lease (taking into account average dead times when the equipment is not leased) exceeds the payments on the equipment loan. When you are a large corporation, these issues are not such a big deal. When you are a start-up, however, you must manage the cash flow very carefully, not overdoing things prematurely to drive your bank account to zero before the next infusion comes in (either in the form of a new investment or profits from the revenue stream).

In order to overcome this cash flow issue, many companies that use a SaaS business model require that their customers pay the subscription fee one year in advance. In this scenario, the cash flow issue is not as bad and actually provides the supplier with much needed working cash twelve months in advance (minus the time delay in the invoice payment terms).

PC Open System Model

Another modern-day example of a platform model is the IBM (NYSE:IBM) personal computer (PC). Back in the day, "IBM" was almost synonymous with "computer." Their market share of all computers sold was 60 percent in 1970, but that figure dropped to 32 percent in 1980, mainly due to the growing popularity of minicomputers (which IBM didn't make) and, to some extent, of microcomputers (an older word for personal computers). The microcomputers market was dominated by the Commodore PET, Atari 8-bit family, Apple II, Tandy Corporation's TRS-80, and various CP/M machines. Total microcomputer industry revenue was $150 million by 1979, with annual growth more than 40 percent.

IBM had to do something drastic to regain their dominance, and they did—but not without a struggle. The incubation of IBM's microcomputer, or PC, was embroiled in lots of internal political agony. As in any large corporation, some executives opposed the new idea for fear of product cannibalism—of their mainframe business. (Others opposed the new PC because it wasn't considered a dignified enough product for the industry giant.)

> **Lesson 1:** Don't let inside politics handicap innovation. Throughout the years I worked at Motorola, innovation was always suffering from in-house politics, especially the fear of new products cannibalizing the old.

The main innovation in the IBM PC was not in the technology, but rather in the business model. Talking from strictly a technology point of view, IBM lagged behind when it came to microcomputers. In an unprecedented strategic decision, IBM's leadership decided to open up their incipient PC's design and architecture to third-party players. This created a tremendous tailwind that propelled IBM's penetration of the PC market. One year after their PC's release, *PC World* reported that 753 software packages were available for it—more than four times the number available for the Apple Macintosh one year after its release. An entire subindustry soon formed around IBM's PC open system, which became the de facto standard microcomputer.

> **Lesson 2:** An ecosystem tailwind is crucial to commercialization success. Multiple entities in the ecosystem are motivated to help you create such a boost for your business because you all will benefit from a successful outcome. Do not resent other businesses making money by partnering with you. You can't do it all. The ecosystem support will more than compensate you for giving up slices of your pie to them.

The purpose of these different platform business model possibilities is to make it easier for the customer to attain your product or service. Like individuals, corporations may have different preferences as far as the trade-offs between the different business models. The best strategy is to be flexible about the business model you choose and accept any engagement model that is convenient for your customer.

The advantage of the linear business model is its simplicity: You pay for what you buy. It's simple for customers to understand what they're paying for and even simpler for suppliers to quantify the give and take for themselves, and thus the ROI.

The variations of the platform business model are endless.

And just like IBM did when developing its PC, the success of your new product or service could definitely stem from innovating a business model no one thought about before.

---

e-commerce Model

It's somewhat of a challenge to categorize e-commerce as a different business model. e-commerce is more about the technology and venue of the business transaction, not a business model by itself. It could be a linear model if you just pay for an item you buy—such as buying a book on Amazon (NASDAQ: AMZN), for example. On the other hand, a platform business model may occur in an e-commerce venue.

Let's look now at an example of an e-commerce platform business model.

China's e-commerce market is dominated by Alibaba (NYSE:BABA). While Amazon replicated the large centralized mall retail model typical to Western societies, China in the 1990s had mainly mom-and-pop stores, no large shopping centers or malls.[3] Alibaba's original idea was to create a global marketplace that would connect small Chinese businesses with the world's buyers.

Though the company operates through a unique combination of business models, Alibaba's core business resembles that of eBay.[4] Alibaba acts as a middleman between buyers and sellers online, and it facilitates the sale of goods between the two parties through its extensive network of websites. Its largest site, Taobao, operates as a fee-free marketplace where neither sellers nor buyers are assessed a fee for completing transactions. Rather, the millions of active sellers on Taobao pay a fee to rank higher on the site's internal search engine, generating advertising revenue for Alibaba that resembles Google's core business model.

Alibaba was determined to block eBay (NASDAQ: EBAY) from entering the Chinese market. Yet, at the time of its inception, Alibaba was tiny compared to the mighty eBay. After all, the U.S. auction service wasn't Chinese and didn't understand the Chinese markets like Alibaba did. For example, eBay cut back on features that Chinese consumers liked, such as emoticons and animations. Taobao ramped these features up to become a far more social commerce model, which added to the perception that the service was free. eBay didn't offer a free version, so it couldn't compete, and it made other mistakes. It eventually pulled out of China completely, having lost millions of dollars. By that point, Alibaba knew it had won, and it began to diversify into other areas. For example, Alipay was launched in 2004 as an escrow account service to allow consumers to hold funds until they were happy with the goods they received. This was key to Taobao's growth, as China had very poor consumer protection laws. In November 2017, Alibaba's market value was assessed as $490 billion, Amazon's as $570 billion, and eBay's as $37 billion.

Takeaways

- The linear business model is not dead. In fact, in many businesses (your local supermarket, liquor store, and shoe store, to name a few), it is still the most commonly used model in day-to-day life.

- Variations of the platform business model have become more popular in recent years. Among the core model's advantages is the favorable tailwind it creates in the ecosystem and the flexibility it offers to your customers.

- When you think about your new product, add the business model conversation to the discussion because complex platform business models require more time in which to sign up the proper third parties.

- Start-up businesses must remember to consider the cash flow impact of the business model they choose.

CHAPTER 8

TECHNOLOGY AND R&D

As we have seen already, many things happen in parallel in the life of a business, and many topics are interrelated. That's why I am covering the same topic in multiple locations with a different focus each time. It is never a clear-cut sequence, so don't be concerned that as you generate innovative ideas and pursue developing selected ones that you are not following a linear path in sequential steps along a straight line.

R&D is one of those interrelated topics. Remember that this critical part of any venture has been discussed in the context of budgeting R&D as you evaluate new product ideas (chapter 4); of funding a new product or service (chapter 10); and of preparing to launch and market a new product or service (chapter 12). Wow! Here, in this chapter, the context is managing the R&D process as a whole.

Before I proceed, however, please indulge me in presenting a short primer on what I mean, exactly, by calling this chapter "Technology and R&D."

Innovation Primer for Nonscientists

"Science" is defined as "a systematic enterprise that creates, builds, and organizes knowledge in the form of testable explanations and predictions." "Technology" is defined as "the application of knowledge for practical purposes."

Science may be "pure science" pursued for no other reason than the academic curiosity of the researcher. Technology, on the other hand, will take the science along some pragmatic path. For example, if someone develops a method to control the color of eggshells only for the purpose of writing a PhD thesis about it, that's science. If the different colored eggshells turn out to correlate to different nutritional values of the eggs inside them, and they can be productized accordingly (I'm thinking marketable Easter eggs here too), the method becomes a technology.

"Scientific research," or "pure research," implies that it is undertaken with no practical application in mind. On the other hand, "practical research" is usually referred to as the development of technology with some vision of its practical application in mind.

When talking about R&D in the industrial world, "research" is the *development of technology*, while "development" implies *creating a product or a desired outcome* (using given technologies).

Okay, enough about the terminology. In real life, you'll encounter blurry boundaries between these categories. And I'd like to share with you a vivid example of just that.

People often argue that pure research is a waste of money and time. In my opinion, any effort to expand human knowledge will eventually find a practical application that improves human lives.

The NASA program to land on the moon didn't have a practical purpose. But because it required the miniaturization of electronics, we now use and enjoy smart phones (among many other practical products) these many years later. President John F. Kennedy could not have envisioned all the teenagers glued to their smart phones in this twenty-first century when he said on September 12, 1962: "We choose to go to the Moon! We choose to go to the Moon in this decade and do the other things, not because they are easy, but because they are hard; because that goal will serve to organize and measure the best of our energies and skills, because that challenge is one that we are willing to accept, one we are unwilling to postpone, and one we intend to win."

Furthermore, although JFK's main motivation was the strategic competitiveness against the Soviet Union, he saw the potential of the as-yet unidentified good it may bring to humanity and started his speech by saying so.

> "We set sail on this new sea because there is new knowledge to be gained, and new rights to be won, and they must be won and used for the progress of all people. For space science, like nuclear science and all technology, has no conscience of its own. Whether it will become a force for good or ill depends on man, and only if the United States occupies a position of preeminence can we help decide whether this new ocean will be a sea of peace or a new terrifying theater of war."

Later in *Lay an Egg and Make Chicken Soup,* I discuss how large-budget government programs have contributed to the feasibility of commercial applications in later years. But perhaps I've gotten too philosophical here. For now, let's go back to a more practical discussion about how technology and R&D will directly affect your innovative products and services.

"R" = Developing Technology & "D" = Creating Products

Technology, remember, is defined as "the application of knowledge for practical purposes." The term is often perceived to be "high technology," such as computers or cutting-edge medical equipment or procedures, but this is not necessarily the case. History is full of many non-cutting-edge technologies that are often referred to as "low tech," yet they are no less valuable—nor less viable as sources for innovation.

Every technology is actually a facilitating technology. Sometimes the technology is embedded in the product; for example, the semiconductor chip inside your phone. Sometimes the technology facilitates the product but is not embedded in it; for example, a computer software program that generates instructions for what ingredients to mix in baking a cake. The software is not inside the cake, but it facilitated the creation of it. That reminds me of a presentation I heard by a sausage manufacturer who said, depending on what type of meat was used, their software program could calculate the right mix of other ingredients to make each sausage taste the same. The American mystery writer Harlan Coben once said about sausage, "You might like the final taste, but you don't want to see how it was made."

Uber

Another well-known example of a facilitating technology that is not embedded inside the end product is ridesharing services such as Uber and Lyft.

Uber is considered to be the ridesharing pioneer; however, what most Millennials don't realize is that the ridesharing concept has existed forever, way before Uber. What Uber brought to the world is automation of the process. It matches drivers and riders based on their location using GPS technology on both parties' mobile phones. And it also uses those phones to process the payment at the end of the ride. Uber didn't invent any breakthrough technology. It integrated existing technologies to introduce a breakthrough service.

Similarly, crowdsourcing has become very popular in recent years, as have crowd fed GPS like Waze and home rental applications such as Airbnb and Home Away.

Gutenberg's Printing Press Facilitates Religious Education

Here is a radical example from the end of the medieval era showing how one technology invention indirectly contributed to a different product.

During the Middle Ages in western Europe, Christians followed a version of the Christian Bible that had been translated into Latin and painstakingly copied by hand. Despite the prevalent use of the Latin language in Roman Catholic services, most Medieval Europeans were illiterate, unable to understand the liturgy. During church services, most people looked at the images in the stained glass windows and on the walls. These pictures illustrated the Bible stories for the people in the audience.

Johannes Gutenberg's invention of the printing press around 1448 had a significant impact on the spread of ideas in Europe and beyond. Printing technology traveled quickly across the continent and, at a time of great religious change, played a key role in the success of the Protestant Reformation.

Reformation leader Martin Luther could preach only to a limited number of people, but the printed word could spread his message to many more.

The printing press drastically cut the cost of producing books and other written materials. Gutenberg did not invent God, nor the Reformation movement, but his invention of the mechanical printing press facilitated the widespread dissemination of religious knowledge from a few exclusive church leaders of the traditional religious establishments to the masses.

As a tool for the distribution of knowledge, the invention of the printing press in the 1500s is analogous to the Internet of the 1990s.

Beer—New Taste, Old Tech

The word "technology" is often synonymous with "cutting edge." This is a misconception. "Technology" doesn't have to be cutting edge. "Technology" is the basic know-how that facilitates a product. Fermentation is the technology behind beer, and it's been around for 10,000 years! (The earliest known chemical evidence of barley beer dates to circa 3500–3100 BC from the site of Godin Tepe in the Zagros Mountains of Western Iran.[1] The *Epic of Gilgamesh* also made reference to the consumption of beer.)

That said, however, its lineage as the world's oldest prepared beverage doesn't mean there's no room for additional business innovations and new products based on that old technology.

The beer industry exceeds $500 billion these days, and it is still growing at 6 percent per year.[2] How come? The continuous growth of the beer market can be largely credited to new developments for specific tastes and preferences as well as different ways to experience beer. By that, I mean everything from the emergence in the 1930s of the first sports bars to the proliferation of microbreweries and brewpubs—beginning in the 1970s in the UK and, a decade later, in the USA. A classic example of a somewhat recent development in the low-technology beer industry is "light beer." Though the term is familiar, not very many could tell you that Joseph Lawrence Owades (July 9, 1919–December 16, 2005) is the father of light beer.

Owades' ideas on the nature of yeast metabolism and the starches found in malt led him to search for (and ultimately create) an enzyme that could break the side-branching chains of starch. This allowed yeast to digest all the starch and produce a beer with no residual carbohydrates (and thus fewer calories) while still maintaining an acceptable alcohol content. Owades' company at the time, Rheingold, introduced the first light beer in 1967, called Gablinger's Diet Beer. As so often happens, however, this first product did not succeed. The recipe and brand for low-calorie beer changed several hands, until it was finally sold to Miller Brewing Company in 1972. Miller Lite was introduced nationally in 1975. Miller's heavy-advertising approach worked where the two previous light beers had failed, and Miller's early production totals of 12.8 million barrels quickly increased to 24.2 million barrels by 1977 as the company rose to second place in the American brewing marketplace. Other brewers responded. In particular, Anheuser-Busch (NYSE:BUD). It heavily advertised its Bud Light in 1982, which eventually overtook Miller Lite in sales by 1994. The global light beer market has boomed to more than $100 billion.[3]

Although Owades might not have become as rich as Rockefeller from the sale of his light beer, he nevertheless held many patents and received the 1994 Award of Merit from the Master Brewers Association of the Americas. He was among those awarded the Sesquicentennial Medal as a distinguished alumnus by NYU Polytechnic University. He wrote the articles on beer and alcohol metabolism for the *Encyclopedia of Food Science and Technology*, and he was named to the Board of the American Committee for the Weizmann Institute of Science in Israel, where in 1999 he endowed the Joseph and Ruth Owades Chair in Chemistry. (My small personal connection to the story: During my high school days, I spent my summers working as a lifeguard at the Weizmann Institute's swimming pool. Beer was a common hydration source among us lifeguards back then, but I don't remember Joseph Owades ever stopping by with free samples from his lab.)

The moral of this story is threefold:

1. **Often the first pioneer doesn't succeed.** It may require a heavy-duty player with deep pockets to propel a new product category. As I've mentioned earlier, the same thing happened with personal computers; they became pervasive only after IBM entered the game. This also happened with light beer; it became a success only after Miller acquired the rights to the technology.

2. **A good product is not enough.** An aggressive marketing campaign is needed to accelerate the adoption.

3. **You can do very well developing products based on old technologies.** One big advantage is that you minimize the technology risk.

Managing the R&D Process

Complex projects with diverse disciplines could easily get out of control if not managed properly. The array of R&D activities is no exception.[4] The primary challenge of project management is to achieve all the project goals within the given constraints. These goals are usually described in project documentation created at the beginning of the development process. The primary constraints are scope, time, quality, and budget. A project manager on staff, with the responsibility of planning, executing, and controlling the project, must be assigned to large multifaceted projects.

Project management is a separate management discipline with its own certification. The most common type of certification is the Project Management Professional (PMP) offered by the Project Management Institute (PMI), a not-for-profit professional membership association for the project management profession. One of the main competencies a project manager must have is risk management. Too many things can go wrong in complex projects, and the project plan must address the most critical ones with proper mitigation plans in place. When you build a house, schedule slippage is an inconvenience. In the competitive world of who will be first to market with a new product, schedule slippage could have a significant impact on the success of the new product and the financial performance of the company.

We need look no further than the Boeing's (NYSE:BA) Dreamliner to see live and in color the manifestation of the project manager's saying, "Anything that can go wrong will go wrong."[5]

The original schedule called for Boeing's 787 Dreamliner to be unveiled in 2008, but the first actual delivery was made three full years behind schedule. These delays came from multiple directions: supply chain shortages, software bugs, and labor strikes. The postponements caused three types of financial aftershocks: delayed revenues due to delayed deliveries, order cancellations, and late fines Boeing was required to pay to the impacted customers.

This three-year delay, with the average unit cost of a single aircraft being approximately $250 million, cost Boeing approximately $10 billion in annual revenue shortfall. That's not chump change.

Takeaways

- "Research" is development of technology, while "development" implies creation of a product.

- While pure research may start with an unknown practical application, it often leads to one sometime later.

- Complex projects with a diversity of disciplines could easily get out of control if not managed properly. The primary challenge of project management is to achieve all the project goals within the given constraints.

PART IV

FUND THE CHICKEN

"Money makes the world go 'round."

—John Kander, composer, songwriter

CHAPTER 9

FINANCIAL MODELING AND EVALUATION

Financial modeling is an important tool throughout the life cycle of a business, with special significance to new products planning and execution. "Financial modeling" is a general, somewhat loose term that refers to any mathematical model designed to represent (a simplified version of) the financial performance of a business or a project. Before any project centered on a new product starts, the financial model is the tool used to evaluate the economics of the new product. As the project enters its execution stages, the financial model serves as a tracking tool to assess the progress of the project vis-à-vis the original plan. As the project progresses, some of the assumptions about the product should be replaced by facts, thus guaranteeing that the financial model is a better reflection of the reality in the marketplace.

In this chapter, I introduce you to the two main components of any financial modeling. Then, I show you how best to use that financial modeling to evaluate the economic health of each and every new product or service you'll create at your company.

The Sales Forecast

One critical component in any financial modeling is the sales forecast. To refresh your memory, you might want to review the details about this subject in chapter 5, "Estimating Demand for a New Product." In that chapter, I described different methodologies to use in developing the sales forecast. Here in this chapter, I am spending a little more time on how best to handle the data that was developed in the sales forecast.

The important thing to track is the set of assumptions that created the sales forecast. At some point, investors or management would like to run different scenarios based on different assumptions, and it is important to track what assumptions drove plan A versus which assumptions drove plan B, and so on. The different scenarios may be a result of different forecasting methodologies and/or different assumptions the sales forecast is based on. Although the different methodologies and different assumptions create a range of results, it also improves the confidence level in these results and helps you understand the possibility of options in front of you.

As the new product starts to be accepted in the market, the actual sales numbers may help you fine-tune the sales forecast based on initial actual sales, thus further increasing the confidence level in the model.

The Manufacturing Plan

Once the sales forecast is understood, the second component is the manufacturing plan. Although the manufacturing plan is driven by the sales forecast, it must also take into account the company's manufacturing cycle time and inventory policy. If, for instance, you plan to sell 10,000 units during the first month of introduction and the manufacturing cycle time is three months, you must start building those 10,000 units three months before launch. So far, it is simple to understand. For a start-up company, however, such aggressive sales growth (10,000 units is nothing to sneeze at) may cause a significant cash gap. In the sample spreadsheet that follows, my sales forecast for a hypothetical start-up came up with selling 1,000 units in month one, 10,000 in the second month, 30,000 in the third month, and 50,000 units in each of the three months thereafter. The manufacturing cost is $10. The selling price is $25. For simplicity, let's assume the cash transaction happens at the same time as the accounting department's recognition of the transaction.

	Month –3	Month –2	Month –1	Month 1	Month 2	Month 3
Unit Sales	0	0	0	1,000	10,000	30,000
Revenue	0	0	0	25,000	250,000	750,000
Manufacturing Units	1,000	10,000	30,000	50,000	50,000	50,000
Manufacturing Cost	10,000	100,000	300,000	500,000	500,000	500,000
Cash Balance	–10,000	–100,000	–300,000	–475,000	–250,000	250,000
Cumulative Cash Balance	–10,000	–110,000	–410,000	–885,000	–1,135,000	–885,000

Notice that in this simple example, although month 3 is the first profitable month, the accumulated cash deficit from the prior six months is still significant and the negative cash hole at the end of month 3 is $885,000. As we see in the bottom line of month 2, the start-up has to reserve $1.135 million to fund the manufacturing launch ramp. In a large corporation, this phenomenon is not a major one in management's overall decision-making. A start-up company, however, must plan for it, and the proper amount of funding must be raised ahead of time to cover this period of disconnect.

This spreadsheet is a simplified example to demonstrate the cash flow gap created by aggressive growth. In real life, the financial modeling can get very complex very quickly. Just think about multiple products, each with its own sales forecast and its own supply chain complexities and cost structure. Add to that employees' payroll (each one with a different base salary and different incentive package); multiple lines for general and administrative (G&A) expenses such as rent, phone bills, G&A payroll; legal fees; marketing and sales, each with its own, different pay structure; marketing campaign costs; different countries with different currency dependencies, taxes; and so on. Last but not least, do not forget to take into account the fact that you need to continue to fund the business during the chasm period.[1] (See more about the gap between initial funding and cash flow in chapter 11, "Business Development.")

The financial modeling is pretty complex even for a small start-up company. The common practice is to have each department (or discipline) detailed in a separate tab of the spreadsheet and to just link the top page to the bottom line of that department's tab. The higher-level model should show one line for each department, with the details laid out in the departmental tabs.

Once the basic model is established, you can start to look at sensitivities and potential bottlenecks in the business. Ask questions such as these to determine what those sensitivities and bottlenecks are:

- What if sales will be 20 percent less than projected?
- What if the launch date is delayed by three months?
- What if production costs will be 50 percent higher?
- What if competitive pressure will force us to reduce pricing by 15 percent?
- What if the currency of my home country will devalue relative to the currency of my largest international supplier?

At a minimum, you must run through each of these worst-case scenarios, one by one, and make sure the business will survive.

This model also helps evaluate the value of the business a few years out, because the main goal of the entrepreneurs and their investors is to sell the business at a huge profit five to seven years later (i.e., exit).

Evaluate the New Product's Economic Health

Now that you've put together the two key components of financial modeling—sales forecast and manufacturing plan—let's take a look at several methods to evaluate the economic health of a new product proposal. These are net present value and internal rate of return (both of which were described briefly in chapter 4, "Evaluating New Product Ideas") as well as payback period and VC exit. The common thread among the different comparison methods in the descriptions that follow is the fact that financial transactions are time dependent. One hundred dollars today is not the same as what one hundred dollars will be a year from now.

Net Present Value (NPV)

NPV is a measurement of profit calculated by subtracting the present values (PVs) of cash outflows (including initial costs) from the PVs of cash inflows over a period of time.

Each cash inflow and outflow is discounted back to its PV. Then all are summed.

$$\frac{R_t}{(1 + i)^t}$$

Therefore, NPV is the sum of all terms, where

R_t = the net cash flow (i.e., cash inflow/cash outflow at time t)

i = the discount rate (i.e., the return that could be earned per unit of time on an investment with similar risk)

t = the time of the cash flow

$$NPV(i, N) = \sum_{t=0}^{N} \frac{R_t}{(1 + i)^t}$$

Many computer-based spreadsheet programs have a built-in formula for the PV and the NPV.

The NPV exercise brings all the transactions to a single point in time—the present so an apples-to-apples comparison can be made. In most cases, it is investment at the present time compared to payback in the future.

Internal Rate of Return (IRR)

The IRR on an investment or project is the annualized effective compounded return rate, or rate of return, that sets the NPV of all cash flows (both positive and negative) from the investment equal to zero. IRR is another tool that facilitates comparison between transactions that happen at different points in time.

Given the (period, cash flow) pairs (n, Cn), where there is a positive integer, the total number of periods N, and the NPV, the IRR is given by the following:

$$NPV = \sum_{n=0}^{N} \frac{C_n}{(1 + r)^n} = 0$$

Payback Period

The payback period is the length of time required to recover the cost of an investment. The payback period of a given investment or project is a quick determinant of whether to undertake the position or project. The payback period ignores the time value of money, unlike other methods of capital budgeting such as NPV or IRR.

In some industries, the payback period is a commonly used as a rule of thumb for a quick evaluation of a project proposal.

Example: If I need to invest €1 million in my building in order to save €100 thousand per year in my energy costs, the payback period is said to be ten years. There are no hard rules here. It is about the tolerance and patience of the decision maker. In some cases, people will look for three-year payback periods; in other cases, twenty years will be enough. It is totally subjective. As a supplier, you must know the preferred payback period of your customers so you will know how to assess your own proposition and its potential to be accepted.

A VC Firm's Exit

VC firms manage limited duration funds and expect to achieve meaningful returns to the fund investors within five to seven years. Keep in mind that a venture investment is usually not liquid during the holding period; thus, a liquidation (or exit) goal is set to allow the investors (be they individuals or such large financial institutions as pension funds, banks, or mutual funds) to cash out (hopefully with significant profit).

No matter how extensive the due diligence process is, history shows that an early-stage venture fund is going to experience a loss from one-third of their investment portfolio, a breakeven from one-third, and substantial returns from one-third. The fund aims to get a 3 times gross return (which, with the usual fee structure, translates into 15 percent to 25 percent IRR, depending on the actual timing of the cash flows).

A "home run" return is when a single company returns the entire fund. A meaningful return occurs when a company returns about one-third of the fund.

There are two schools of thought regarding the best strategy for selecting venture investments (and both of them have been proven successful): Some VC firms will aim only at potential home runs, knowing that some of those investments will most likely end up being just a meaningful exit or even fail. Other VC firms will mainly aim at potential meaningful exits, expecting that one or two of these investments will end up being a home run.

The potential exit value can be estimated by looking at the revenue and profit targets of the company and the valuation multipliers for that industry.

Not every company can grow quickly enough to generate venture-scale returns. The growth potential is determined by market size, product acceptance, competition, and the ability of the company to execute such an aggressive growth path.

One can work backward to find out the growth rates required to hit that meaningful exit target.

With the financial modeling fresh in your mind, it's a good time to consider where to find funding—the options are many—for your new product or service. That's the subject of the next chapter.

Takeaways

- The financial complexity of even a small start-up requires substantial financial modeling in order to evaluate the economics of the project and later on monitor its execution.

- The attractiveness of a new product proposal depends on the goals of the funding source and the industry. Several methods were reviewed: NPV, IRR, pay back period, and VC firm's exit goals. Each of these criteria may result in either a go or no-go vote for the project.

CHAPTER 10

FUNDING FOR A NEW PRODUCT OR SERVICE

You have a great idea, but it takes time and money to implement.

The time factor could be critical for a couple of reasons. The longer it takes to develop a product, the more likely that your competitors will have a similar or an alternative idea and beat you to the market. (Recall the example of Toyota's capture of the market given in chapter 1, "Why Innovate?") More time usually implies that more money will be needed to fund the implementation process. A second time-related element may be in a defined window of opportunity. For instance, if your new product is targeted for the Christmas season and you miss that season, you lose an entire year. If you target a new service for a big once-in-a-lifetime concert but you weren't ready on that date, you missed that particular opportunity completely. (Think the Beatles' final live concert in San Francisco's Candlestick Park on August 29, 1966 or U2's thirtieth anniversary tour in 2017 of *The Joshua Tree*'s release.)

Many engineers and scientists think that if they get their prototype to work in the lab, their job is done. This is a huge mistake—albeit a common one—because it takes additional time and funding to move the cost and manufacturability as well as the marketing and business development investment along the learning curve.

The market adoption time has additional funding-related implications: A proof of market acceptance is often required before supplemental funding kicks in. It is quite common for customers to use the new products in ways that were not tested in the lab, thus uncovering unexpected product faults, which require additional time and additional funding to repair.

In the start-up world, it is quite common to fund a company in phases. This is the investors' way to manage risk. The terms of an investment contract between investors and the company often include (in addition to the amount of the initial investment) future milestones that will trigger infusions of more money.

In large corporations, there is a time-sensitive element that needs to be planned for as well. Namely, most companies review their budget annually. In the case of multi-year projects, the project managers will have to renegotiate their budget every year during the budget planning cycle.

Corporate Creation or Entrepreneurial Initiative?

Many good groundbreaking products—such as hybrid cars, cellular phones, Apple iPads and iPods, to name but a few—started in large corporations, while other services, like social media and e-commerce, started as entrepreneurial initiatives. Each approach has its pros and cons. Large corporations are usually slower to buy into a radical initiative. Once they do, however, they invariably have all the resources to make it a success.

Entrepreneurs have a much faster decision-making process and therefore can kick-off the new venture much quicker. Nevertheless, they often lack the resources to execute freely and rapidly and depend on interim funding from outside investors.

Oftentimes, start-ups start their journey when a corporate executive with an idea for a new business tries to promote his idea inside his own firm and gets frustrated by the internal bureaucracy and mountains of hurdles he needs to jump through to make it happen.

Ross Perot was a successful IBM salesperson when he came up with the idea of outsourcing IT services in the late 1950s. He tried to promote this idea inside IBM first but was ignored by his supervisors. He left IBM in 1962 to found Electronic Data Systems Corporation (EDS), which built and ran data processing systems for other companies and organizations. In 1984, General Motors (NYSE:GM) bought a controlling interest in EDS for $2.4 billion.

Established companies normally set aside a certain percentage of revenue earmarked for R&D for new products and services. The decision-making process usually starts once a year during the budget planning cycle. The implementation process will vary depending on the industry, the type of products and services, and the specific company's culture and procedures. In large corporations, the variety of options for new products to enter into the implementation process is endless.

Funding Sources for Entrepreneurs

There are diverse finance regulations in different countries. In this chapter, I've tried to be as generic and country independent as possible, but by no means have I covered all the possible options around the globe. So, I highly recommend that you research the financial and legal systems in your specific location when it comes to these sources of equity. Dealing with governments is never simple, and many countries have several agencies that regulate financial investments. The most relevant agency in the United States, for instance, is the Securities and Exchange Commission (SEC). Among numerous other examples are the Swiss Financial Market Supervisory Authority (FINMA), the China Securities Regulatory Commission (CSRC), the Securities and Commodities Authority (SCA) in the United Arab Emirates, and the Comissão de Valores Mobiliários (CVM) in Brazil. I highly recommend that you hire an attorney who specializes in private investment regulations in your country who will guide you through the process and supply you with all the required documentation.

Bootstrapping

Entrepreneurs are said to be bootstrapping, or self-funding, when they have founded and built their business from personal finances alone, without taking outside capital.

The main benefit of bootstrapping is the ability to maintain control over all the decisions. The downside, however, is that this form of financing places additional financial risk on the entrepreneur. It also may cause delays to the launch because, more often than not, the bootstrapping entrepreneur doesn't have sufficient funding to hire the required team and is trying to do it all by him- or herself. Bootstrapping makes sense only if your own finances are more than sufficient to fund the business. Do not fall into the trap of trying to keep 100 percent equity at all costs and run the risk of not having enough money to support the business.

Possible Self-Funding Options

The term "self-funding" doesn't necessarily mean the cash in your day-to-day checking account. Let's review a few options that fall under that rubric.

- You might draw on personal savings but don't risk it all. Budget a certain percentage of your personal savings, and if it is not enough then seek additional outside sources. If the personal savings you plan to use are in a retirement account, you may need to pay taxes and/or a penalty for the early withdrawal, depending on the type of account and on your age.

- You might be able to self-fund your own enterprise if

your spouse or partner earns enough to provide for daily household needs. For example, my wife started her interior design business, ELB-Design, while I was working full-time as an executive at Motorola. This gave her breathing room to ramp up her business without the need for additional capital.

- You could consider gradually starting your own business in your spare time while you still have a job that puts food on the table and shelter over your head.

- You might think about obtaining a part-time job or a consulting gig that will give you some income while leaving enough spare time to work on your new venture.

- You might be eligible for a Rollover for Business Start-ups (ROBS); just beware that this option is not available in all countries. This route allows you to instruct your retirement fund to invest in your own business. Certain rules and regulations apply depending on the country and on your age.

These are the main equity sources from which to choose if you take the bootstrapping (i.e., self-funding) route. Study each option and select one or a combination of the above options for your start-up.

Debt

An alternative to equity funding is to take out a loan. The advantage of a loan is that you do not give up equity in the new business. The disadvantages are twofold, though: the interest to be paid for the privilege of borrowing the money, and the amount of the loan may be limited to the collateral the entrepreneur is able to provide.

Let's review a few channels through which you might secure a loan (and therefore incur debt).

- **Banks:** Banks will require some collateral for the loan. If the new business has some traction already, the bank may loan you a certain percentage of your backlog and will take the accounts receivable as collateral.

- **Credit cards:** This is an easy route if you have already qualified for a credit card with a high enough credit limit to suffice for your business start-up needs. Some credit cards offer very attractive introductory rates, which could be a good cheap source of cash.

- **Home equity loan:** Depending on the equity you have in your house and on the regulations in your region, you may be able to take additional mortgage on your house. This means that you use the equity on your house as collateral for the loan.

- **Personal loan:** A relatively new option is peer-to-peer (P2P) lending, through which people either borrow or lend money without a financial institution being involved. P2P sites harness both technology and big data for the purpose of connecting borrowers to investors faster and cheaper than traditional banks can.

- **Small Business Administration (SBA) loan:** The U.S. government encourages entrepreneurship and will lend you money to start your business. Visit https://www.sba.gov/funding-programs/loans for information on how to apply for a loan and what the terms of the loan will be.

To summarize: Incurring debt could complement other forms of funding. It depends on whether you qualify for a certain type of loan, whether you are applying for a reasonable amount, and whether you are willing to pay the interest required.

Friends & Family

Friends and family could be a great source of funds to kick-start a business. This route can be in the form of a loan or an equity investment. Heed the old saying, however, that warns, "If you lend money to a friend, you will lose the money and lose the friend." Just be careful not to ruin your relationships because of it. You can minimize the chances that the deal will result in the loss of money and friendship by documenting *everything* and having both parties sign those documents. The main problem usually occurs in repaying the money. To what extent will you give your friend extensions? Will you sue your friend if he is dragging his feet in paying back the loan? It's a personal decision that you should make cautiously.

Government Grant

Governments around the globe recognize that entrepreneurship is a good source of economic growth, and they offer different grant programs to encourage it. Check the rules and regulations and the fine print regarding each of these programs. This could be an especially attractive route because many government programs don't require equity, nor do they charge interest. They usually have some other strings attached, though, so read carefully. Strings may be in the form of how many employees you have to hire, quotas on the types of employees you must hire (based on such factors as gender, minorities, veterans), location limits, intellectual property limits, matching rules, and so on. There are hundreds of plans, each with its specific purpose and limitations. Just make sure that you understand your obligations if you accept a grant and that these obligations are something you can live with. Note also that some of these government grants may apply to established companies as well as to start-ups.

Crowdfunding

This is the practice of funding a project or venture by raising many small amounts of money from a large number of people, typically via the Internet. In 2015, it was estimated that worldwide more than $34 billion had been raised through crowdfunding.

There are two main types of crowdfunding:

1. **Presell the product or service to launch a business.** Since the buyers take a risk in pre-buying a product before it is even fully designed and proven, it is a common practice either to offer the products at a significantly deep discount or to add to the offering some enticing perks beyond the basic product.

2. **The backers receive shares of a company in exchange for their money.** If you consider investing via this route, be aware that some of the crowdfunding vehicles don't do any due diligence on the offering; thus, you may want to do your own research. (Note: OurCrowd— www.ourcrowd.com—which I am a limited partner

with, provides the vehicle for crowdfunding investment while also doing due diligence like any other normal VC firm would.)

Although the term "crowdfunding" is relatively new, the principles of this practice reach as far back as early-1700s Ireland, when Jonathan Swift, dubbed "the father of microcredit," founded the Irish Loan Fund. The fund provided small loans to low-income, rural families with no collateral or credit history.

In honor of Jonathan Swift's pioneering of crowdfunding, we will stay on the British Isles for the following contemporary example.

GlenWyvis, the world's first community-owned gin and whisky distillery, raised more than £2.6 million from some 2,600 investors and contributors in its first Open Share Offer in 2016. Based in the northern Highlands town of Dingwall, Scotland, construction on the distillery started some ninety years after the region's last distillery closed down.[1]

Investments of more than £750 conferred shares and part ownership. At the top of the list are three crowdfunders who invested more than £50,000 each.

In order to incentivize investors and to compensate for the early-stage risk, rewards for the many small investors included bottles of gin (which can be produced instantly while waiting for the whisky to mature), whisky bottles starting in 2020, casks filled with whisky, whisky tours, helicopter tours from the Flying Farmer himself, and more.

Strategic Partnership

A strategic partner could be a supplier, a distributor, or a customer who sees the value of your new solution and is willing and able to help foot the bill, or at least part of it.

If your new product or service solves a painful B2B problem that the market craves a solution to, there might be potential early adopters who could make a strategic investment if they think you have a good chance at relieving their pain. Sometimes they might do it because it gives them a competitive advantage against their competitors.

Asking a customer who is also a strategic partner to become an investor brings with it several very important benefits:

1. It will provide you with real, honest customer feedback during the project. It is one thing to get a customer's feedback in a noncommittal meeting; the feedback is much more reliable when this customer is also an investor.

2. It is a very strong signal to other investors that your idea is valid, thus making it easier to raise additional money.

3. It is likely, if you execute well, that a strategic investor will provide the start-up with an exit path later on. It is their way to get their foot in the door on this new idea without risking too much money initially. But once the idea proves to be successful, they will buy the company.

For the strategic partner—normally a larger corporation—this venue provides access to innovation that will take longer to implement internally because of the inherent longer bureaucracies and decision-making processes in large companies.

Barter

Start-ups can reduce some of the funding they need by bartering services in return for equity. Here's a simple example. Buy legal services at a reduced rate and in return provide the attorney with equity in the company. The same type of bartering can be arranged with accountants, realtors, and so on. This requires significant negotiation with all these service providers, however, who may not necessarily see the value of an early-stage equity or are not willing to absorb the risk in bartering over against stable predetermined fees. Many start-ups barter labor costs by granting employees stock options and in return get them to work for a reduced paycheck (this is called "sweat equity"). Some incubators and accelerators (see the following example) bundle several services for their portfolio start-up companies in return for equity.

Angel Investors

Angel investors are individuals who invest in start-ups, usually at an early stage, to help them take their first steps.

These are affluent individuals who inject capital for start-ups in exchange for ownership equity or convertible debt. Some angel investors invest through crowdfunding platforms online or build angel investor networks to pool their capital.

Unlike venture capitalists that take pooled money from many other investors and place it in a strategically managed fund, angel investors typically use their own money.

Though angel investors usually represent individuals, the entity that actually provides the fund could be a trust, a family fund, or a special purpose partnership between several angel investors, among many other kinds of vehicles.

Since investing in start-up businesses is very high-risk, the effective IRR for a successful portfolio for angel investors ranges from 20 percent to 30 percent. An angel investment will often range from $50 thousand to $1 million, which is more suitable for a seed investment. Most angels will diversify and spread the risk by investing in start-ups from different industries, while others prefer to invest only in businesses in their comfort zone. Most investors specify their investment criteria on their website or social media profile. It will be a waste of time to contact an investor if your start-up is not in his or her areas of focus. Because many of the angel investors are successful businesspeople themselves, the additional benefits to the entrepreneur of partnering with them are the mentorship and business network they bring to the table. Some angels work as executives in relevant potential customer companies and other synergetic businesses, and thus they can open valuable doors for the start-up.

Some angels are organized in angel groups. These groups usually have an application process that must be followed, with certain deadlines for each step in the process. The advantage of applying to a group is the opportunity to pitch to multiple angels simultaneously as well as the potential of receiving a number of checks from several different angels. The main disadvantage is the possibility of a strict schedule of deadlines that are not always in sync with your own. The next submission cycle may be too soon, but the one after that is too late to wait for.

Venture Capitalists

Venture capitalists are private equity investors that provide funding to start-up companies and small businesses. Unlike angel investors, who are individuals, venture capitalists, or venture capital (VC) firms, are institutions that manage a fund.[2]

Once again, since investment in start-ups is very risky, the venture capitalists will look for significantly above-average returns. For new companies or ventures that have yet to generate revenue, VC funding is a popular source for raising capital, especially if they need more funds than they have access to through the other alternatives described in the previous sections.

One important difference between VC and other private equity firms is that VC firms tend to focus on emerging companies that are seeking substantial funds for their early life, while private equity firms normally fund larger, more established companies that are seeking an equity infusion or a chance for the company's founders to cash out from some of their ownership stake.

Most VC firms look to invest in companies that are well managed, have a fully developed business plan, and are poised for substantial growth. Different investors will vary based on such factors as their focused domains, regions, stage of company, and amounts they will invest. In most cases, venture capitalists will prefer to coinvest with other such investors as a way to diversify the risk.

The investors in a VC fund are called "limited partners." These are normally large institutions or high net worth individuals (HNWI), family funds, trusts, and other funds. Since these are private equity investments with no liquidity, the investors expect to cash out on their profits at some point; therefore, a VC fund predefines its life, on average between five and ten years, which means all the companies in the portfolio are expected to have some financial event that will return money to the investors, either as an initial public offering (IPO) or a mergers and acquisitions (M&A) transaction.

As I stated in the section titled "A VC Firm's Exit" in chapter 9, no matter how extensive the due diligence process is, history shows that an early-stage venture fund is going to experience a loss of one-third, a breakeven of one-third, and substantial returns of one-third. Unfortunately, at the beginning of the journey, you don't know which third is which.

Progressive Steps in Engaging Investors

The first step for any business looking for investors is to submit a business plan, either to a VC firm or to an angel investor (or group of angels). The venture capitalists and angels are very busy people. You have a far better chance to be considered if you already know that investor or you are being introduced by a trusted mutual acquaintance. This doesn't guarantee an investment of funds in your business, but it improves the odds that this investor will spend the time to read your material.

The process with investors has several stages. Depending on your prior relationships with the potential investors, though, some stages may be skipped. Generally speaking, however, you need to be ready to go through all of them. Each one of these stages requires different collateral material.

> **Stage one.** Select the right investors. Not all VC firms are created equal. They differ in the focus of their given industry, stage of investment, geography, size of investment, and other considerations. Needless to say, once you have distilled a short

list, make sure the selected VC firms are not already invested in one of your competitors.

When working with a start-up on a fund-raising campaign, I go through the time-consuming process of creating a short list of fewer than two dozen potential investors that are relevant for the particular situation. Once you create the short list, make sure that none of them is already invested in one of your competitors.

Stage two. Fine-tune your elevator pitch to open doors. Investors get many applications every week. These are busy people who don't have time to read them all. They won't even open your attachment if you don't have a kick-ass elevator pitch that will wow them and engage their interest.

Here's the type of elevator pitch I'm talking about:

The next phase of social media will be industry-specific social networks. Currently, Company X is distinguished as a social network that provides the construction industry with a multitude of government-compliant products and services specific to their everyday professional needs!

Company X is growing fast, serving more than 1 million construction professionals. The company signed several monetization partnerships, started revenue this quarter, and is on target to realize its hockey stick $10 million in revenue as early as next year.

Stage three. Be ready to deliver a fast pitch. Many VC firms and angel groups start the process with a speed dating type of event. You get only five or six minutes to tell your story.

Don't try to squeeze thirty minutes' worth of your business plan into this tight time slot. Instead, prepare a short presentation that highlights your main selling points to stimulate your audience's interest to learn more about your venture. If you're successful, you will be invited to a more in-depth meeting. Remember: The goal of this fast pitch is to be invited to the next step in the process.

Stage four. Prepare for an in-depth meeting. Only if you pass through the previous gates will you be invited to a long meeting during which you will get the opportunity to deliver a deep dive about your innovation. Oftentimes, there will be more than one meeting in this stage. Come to these meetings prepared and poised.

Stage five. Go through a due diligence process. Due diligence is a rigorous process of asking questions and reviewing required documents that VC firms collect before making their final decisions related to an investment opportunity. As in every other stage thus far, be prepared to answer their questions and to have the documentation they'll want to review—based on your own due diligence.

Stage six. Understand what a term sheet should contain. Term sheets, at times referred to as memorandums of understanding, serve as a summary of the terms being discussed or offered. The important elements in a term sheet will list the valuation of the company, the money to be invested, the milestone points at which to follow-up investments and/or tranches, the management team, and the board of directors.

Frequently, an acceptance period is mentioned, providing a time frame for a response regarding the information set forth in the term sheets.

I have been involved in the VC investment process numerous times in different capacities: working for VC firms in evaluating business plans; pitching to a VC firm to raise money for start-ups I worked for; and as an intermediary between start-ups and VCs. Most people are not aware that being an intermediary is a time-consuming process. This is not a social event where you casually introduce two people. A formal introduction like this implies that the trusted intermediator gives the start-his blessing. To grant that blessing, an intermediator must be satisfied on at least three fronts:

1. Taking a deep dive into the company's business plan to make sure you understand and believe in it.

2. Sorting through the database of prospective investors to identify the short list of names that can be a potential fit for the company.

3. Reviewing the company's presentation before passing it on to the potential investors. (Most entrepreneurs need help in modifying their documentation to meet investors' high standards.)

The network of contacts I have is very precious to me. I do not want to risk wasting their time. Therefore, I pass each name through the three items in the previous checklist, which is a pretty time-consuming process.

The Unique Place of Incubators and Accelerators in the Life of a Start-Up

A business incubator is an organization that helps start-up companies develop and take their first baby steps by providing different support services and mentorship so the entrepreneurs can focus on execution. Since start-up companies lack resources, experience, and networks, incubators provide services that help them get through initial hurdles in starting up a business. These hurdles include space, funding, legal counsel, accounting, computer services, and other overhead prerequisites to running a business. The incubators make their money by taking equity in the start-ups and/or some nominal monthly fees as well. Some incubators have their own funds to invest in the participating start-ups while others will just provide a network of affiliated investors.

Accelerators are similar to incubators in the type of services they provide. The main difference between the two groups is the duration of the programs they offer. Incubators' programs are longer term, one to two years, while accelerators' programs typically last three to six months.

Allow me to share a great real-world story that demonstrates the effectiveness of using multiple investment sources and showcases an emerging female leader who refused to take "This is a man's work" for an answer.

Biocon

Kiran Mazumdar-Shaw, founder and chairperson of Biocon Limited (BSE: BIOCON), used several of the funding options described previously in her journey to become the richest self-made female in India—and one of the top 50 in the world, with a net worth in excess of $2 billion. I chose her story because you get a firsthand look at several funding sources rolled into one success story.

Mazumdar-Shaw started her career as a trainee brewer in Carlton and United Breweries in Melbourne, Australia, and as a trainee maltster at Barrett Brothers in Burston, Australia. When she investigated the possibility of furthering her career in India, she was told that she would not be hired as a master brewer because "It's a man's work." She did not accept this answer and began to look abroad. Eventually, she was offered a position in Scotland.

Before Mazumdar made that move, however, she met Leslie Auchincloss, founder of Biocon Biochemicals Limited, of Cork, Ireland. Auchincloss's company produced enzymes for use in the brewing, food-packaging, and textile industries. Auchincloss was looking for an Indian entrepreneur to help establish an Indian subsidiary. Mazumdar agreed to undertake the challenge on the condition that if she did not wish to continue after six months, she would be guaranteed a brewmaster's position comparable to the one she was giving up.

After a brief period as a trainee manager for Auchincloss, Mazumdar-Shaw returned to India where she started Biocon India in 1978 in the garage of her rented house in Bengaluru with seed capital of Rs. 10,000 (approximately US $150). Indian laws restricted foreign ownership to 30 percent of the company; thus, the remaining 70 percent was granted to Mazumdar-Shaw.

Initially, she faced credibility challenges because of her young age, her gender, and her innovative business model. Funding was a problem: No bank wanted to lend to her, and a few requested that her father be a guarantor. An accidental meeting with a banker at a social event finally enabled her to get her first financial backing.

One year after its inception, Biocon India was able to manufacture enzymes and to export them to the United States and Europe. At the end of her first year, Mazumdar-Shaw used her earnings to buy a twenty-acre property and dreamed of future expansion.

In 1989, the parent company, Biocon Biochemicals of Ireland, was acquired by Unilever (LSE: ULVR). In 1997, Unilever sold its specialty chemicals division, including Biocon, to Imperial Chemical Industries (ICI, acquired by AkzoNobel in 2007, Euronext: AKZA)). In 1998, Kiran Mazumdar's fiancée, John Shaw, raised $2 million to purchase the outstanding Biocon shares from ICI. The couple married later that year.

In 2004, Mazumdar-Shaw decided to list Biocon on the stock market. The IPO was oversubscribed thirty-three times, and on its first day on the market closed with a value of $1.11 billion. (NSE: BIOCON)

Now that you've got a sense of the type of financial model you'll use in your business, as well as what types of investors you'll approach to secure money for your venture, turn the page to begin the unit that describes how to nurture and monitor your "chicken's" growth.

Takeaways

- Large enterprises have different processes to launch new products internally.

- Start-ups have multiple funding options: self-funding, debt, crowdfunding, government grants, strategic partnerships, and different levels of equity investments (friends and family, angels, and VC firms).

- The main criteria to which type of investment fits best is the amount of money required and the stage of the company.

PART V

PREPARE THE CHICK
FOR SALE

"Growth is never by mere chance;
it is the result of forces working together."
—James Cash Penney, founder, JCPenney

CHAPTER 11

BUSINESS DEVELOPMENT

When the new product is an entire new category, a significantly more substantial effort is required to prepare the ecosystem. Some of this background work is done using marketing tools, but it also requires human intervention to work on the different relationships and supporting deals with a variety of synergistic organizations. That activity is called "business development."

Business development could mean different things to different people (and different industries).

In one of his many contributions to *Forbes* magazine, author Scott Pollack defined business development as "the creation of long-term value for an organization from customers, markets, and relationships."[1] I like Scott's definition but want to simplify it even further: Business development is recruiting the ecosystem to create long-term value for an organization. In this context, "value" is often called a "tailwind."

The Valley of Death

In *Crossing the Chasm: Marketing and Selling Disruptive Products to Mainstream Customers*, author Geoffrey Moore writes in great length about the gap (what he calls the "chasm") or the challenge of acquiring the "early majority" customers.[2] Another term for this phenomenon as applied to start-ups is the "Valley of Death," defined as "that gap between when a company first launches the new product and when it begins generating *steady* revenue from paying customers."[3]

Innovators and early adopters will jump right in because of their curiosity and intellectual interest. Although Moore's book focuses mainly on hi-tech products, the same challenges exist in any new product concept, often even more significantly than in technology.

In many cases, the success of a new product doesn't depend only on the customers' willingness to buy it; other ecosystem players help the market adopt the product. As we just saw in chapter 7, "Business Model," this is especially important when you've followed a complex platform business model in which supplemental ecosystem players provide some of the push effort.

Some businesses with a complex ecosystem—such as the pharmaceutical industry (which I outlined in detail in chapter 7)—must implement extensive business development efforts to succeed. At this point in the discussion, I want to introduce you to one of my clients who bests pharma for complexity.

This particular client was a start-up company that developed an air conditioner add-on device that saves between 20 and 40 percent of the air conditioner's energy consumption. This could mean thousands of dollars in annual savings to a household or millions in yearly savings to corporations housed in large office buildings. On the surface, the device should have been an overnight success. Why was it not? The large number of the start-up's stakeholders and the complexity of the ecosystem slowed down the acceptance significantly.

The list of stakeholders is mind-boggling: shareholders; employees; building owners; building tenants; supply chain of components; third-party sales channels; global multiple utilities that need to recognize the product as an energy-saving device; nonprofit organizations in the green building space that must be convinced the saving potential is real; air-conditioning governing bodies that must approve the required changes in the air-conditioning engineering codes; local governments that don't accept the main governing body's conclusions and thus require additional concerted efforts to be convinced; air-conditioner installers who need to be trained on the new device (and who are not happy to sacrifice short-term billable time for training that may or may not be compensated for when they install the device; and engineering firms that have to be trained on how to design an air-conditioning system that includes this add-on. (Holy mackerel!)

Each one of these stakeholders is led by a different motivation. Businesses driven by money, for instance, will ask whether revenues will go up with this or down. HVAC engineers will wonder if it will increase the complexity of and time spent on their design. The bottom line for almost everyone is whether customers will pay for this extra effort.

Multiply the number of organizations by the diversity of the individuals involved, each with his or her own career aspirations, personality, and risk attitudes, as well as probably politically related motivations. Welcome to the excitement of business development life.

Take heart. What follows is my description of the steps you'll need to take to grow and mature within that life.

Map the Business Ecosystem

The first step in the business development process is always the mapping of the ecosystem, which includes defining the synergistic relationships within the ecosystem and outlining the give-and-take interactions between the players in the space. Here is a generic template you can adapt for your new product or service ecosystem map.

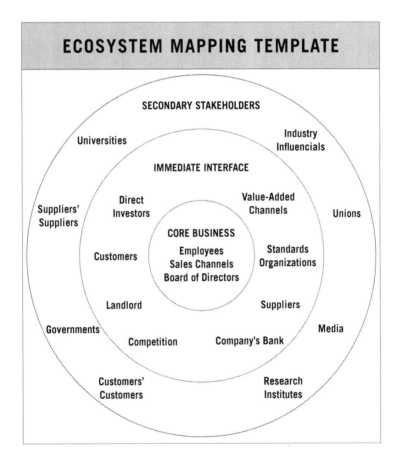

ECOSYSTEM MAPPING TEMPLATE

SECONDARY STAKEHOLDERS

Universities

Industry Influencials

IMMEDIATE INTERFACE

Direct Investors

Value-Added Channels

Suppliers' Suppliers

Unions

CORE BUSINESS

Customers

Employees
Sales Channels
Board of Directors

Standards Organizations

Landlord

Suppliers

Governments

Media

Competition

Company's Bank

Customers' Customers

Research Institutes

Once you populate the template with the individual players in each category, the map becomes exceedingly busy really quickly. (Just look at the air conditioner add-on example mentioned previously.)

Navigate the Ecosystem

The first step was to create the ecosystem map. The next steps are endless. The following sections describe different categories of ecosystem players. The ecosystem map, as its name suggests, is the beginning of a journey toward the desired business outcome. Each business has to define its own business outcome and the strategy to accomplish it. A business outcome may be, for example, "Pass a compatibility test with a synergistic product by a certain date." Another business outcome could be "Have at least three early adopters agree to beta test the prototype." The strategy and action plan to achieve these business outcomes might be totally different and thus may require that different activities take place in the ecosystem.

Examples of Ecosystem Categories

Let's discuss some of these ecosystem categories in detail to help you see the connections and outcomes within the ecosystem more clearly.

Innovators and Early Adopters

The innovators and early adopters are customers that are likely to be the first to jump in and try your new product. It is a good idea to recruit them before the product development even starts. (You'll read much more about early adopters in the next chapter, "Launch Time: Marketing.")

For products that require complex and expensive design efforts (such as a new type of computer or a new restaurant concept), the innovators and early adopters are the first place to validate the new idea (before committing the large amount of design investment required), so you can justify the venture to your superiors, in the case of large companies, or to your investors, if you are an entrepreneur.

In complex B2B situations, the new idea often originates with a customer. Whenever a customer comes to you with a new idea, it is critical that you understand what problem they are trying to solve and that you brainstorm together about the most economical solution. Say that a customer tells you they want to fly from Tokyo to New York in two hours. Your first order of business is to understand why they need to have such a short flight. If you are Boeing, your initial thought will likely be to design a superfast airplane. But a company with keen innovative culture is one that is able to step out of its box and envision a solution to the customer's problem even when it is totally outside the business's perceived mission. Extending its vision, in this case, beyond making airplanes to putting people closer together, through any other technologies that can help achieve that goal.

Is Boeing's business to fly people from point A to point B? Or is it to connect people at point A with people at point B? Maybe a new virtual reality conference capability will be a more economical solution than a new ultrasonic passenger airplane. If you are Boeing, and your initial feasibility study reveals that a two-hour flight from New York to Tokyo is either not feasible or prohibitively expensive, you are likely to return to that customer and say, "Sorry, but we can't do it." On the other hand, an open-minded entrepreneur, with no corporate mission boundaries, may likely approach this need from different angles and different possible technologies, such as a virtual reality conference capability or a life-size videoconference or . . .

Sales Channels

Large companies normally have the channel relationships required to launch a new product. All they need to do is develop the new product training for each particular channel and the incentive campaign to properly compensate the channel for the extra time they need to spend on promoting the new product. (I discuss a lot more about sales in chapter 13.)

Channel development is a major part of business development for start-ups especially. The major channel firms cannot work with every start-up that knocks on their door. They must be convinced that this new product is worth their salespeople's time, the floor space in their warehouse, and their money to purchase inventory in case the channel is a distributer. A better strategy for early-stage start-ups is to recruit sales reps that specialize in emerging new products. Part of the job of these professionals is to further develop the channels and recruit the bigger firms that will eventually add sales power to the start-up.

Governments

Governments usually regulate what they perceive as public health and safety, public interests, and strategic assets preservation.

Whether your new product is in the food, chemicals, or health industries, a big part of your business development activity may require that you deal with government agencies that regulate your industry. A nonhazardous paint in one country may be considered toxic in another country. Organic food is defined differently in different locations. And the list goes on and on.

Other areas that are perceived public interests and are treated differently in different geographies include gambling, sex, alcohol, and drugs to name but a few. A legitimate casino card game in one country may be considered illegal gambling in another.

Governments also regulate business relations to some extent. For example, Uber and Lyft were banned in Austin, Texas, for a long time because the city council viewed them as unfair competition against other forms of public transportation, especially taxis. This disagreement was resolved in 2017.

Standards Organizations

Whenever your new product has to interface with other products in some way or fashion, there is probably at least one standards organization whose specifications you must comply with. Each country has its own such standards organizations. I am talking about standards-setting societies that define the interface between two products that need to work together safely and compatibly. A well-known example is the American Society of Heating, Refrigerating and Air-Conditioning Engineers, better known as ASHRAE, whose mission is to advance the well-being of people worldwide through sustainable technology for the built environment. Other examples include telephones, cable equipment, and something as simple as electrical plugs to fit into an outlet: for example, a 110-volt hair dryer in the United States that requires an adapter for use in Europe, where 220 volts and different physical dimensions of the plug are standard. The International Electrotechnical Commission (IEC) monitors such adapters in its capacity as the world's leading organization that prepares and publishes international standards for all electrical, electronic, and related technologies. There are similar sister organizations in each country.

At a minimum, you must make sure that your new product complies with established standards. A more aggressive approach is to be able to influence the standard in such a way that it will favor your new approach and put some obstacles in the path of your competitors to slow them down. This is a tricky part that requires tremendous political power within a given standards organization. A third possibility concerns cases where the new product is so innovative and extraordinary that it doesn't fall under any of the existing standards. In these cases, a significant part of the business development work is to make sure the relevant standards will be modified to include this new product category. Otherwise, you risk the likely possibility that your new product will be banned for not complying with any standard.

Synergistic Products

The business development activity likewise needs to deal with synergistic products. Obviously, the standards-setting organizations perform some of these tasks, but there are additional activities you must conduct directly with synergistic companies. Such activities serve both as an additional one-on-one test of how well the two products work together and as a way to leverage each product's strengths in co-marketing campaigns, where one plus one is greater than two.

An example of a successful co-marketing campaign was done in 2012 by Taco Bell and Doritos in the fast food–snack food mash-up dubbed "Doritos Locos Tacos."[4]

Taco Bell rolled out its new fast food sensation in March 2012 with a $75 million advertising campaign. They went on to sell a stunning 100 million Doritos Locos Tacos in about ten weeks, making the $1.29 item the largest and most successful product launch in the company's fifty-year history. (In comparison, it took McDonald's, which began slinging fast food in 1958, years to sell that many burgers.)

Part of the business development activity is to identify the synergistic companies that are most compatible with your product and to develop relationships with them in order to perform the co-testing work and later the co-marketing campaigns. In the start-up world, these synergistic companies could turn out to be an exit path in the future, in which the partnering business buys out your entrepreneurial enterprise.

Industry Influencers

Last but not least, you want industry influencers to create a tailwind behind your product. (Recall the complex platform business model section in chapter 7 about the significant role these people play in product launches.) This is very similar to advertising and general public relations, but when the endorsement comes from an industry influencer, it adds so much brand power to the new product. Oftentimes with new consumer products, the industry influencer is a celebrity who will be hired to participate in an ad campaign. A more sophisticated approach is to embed the new product in a new film or reality TV show, or just simply hire a pop star or iconic sports figure to talk about the new product during interviews or speaking engagements.

When it comes to a new complicated B2B offering, industry influencers will not endorse it just for the money, unlike the sports and entertainment celebrities who often promote B2C products. Industry influencers for B2B products are likely to be high-profile university professors or industry gurus. Although they may be looking for some compensation in return for their endorsement, these B2B industry influencers will not risk their professional reputation by endorsing a product they don't truly believe in.

Takeaways

- Business development activity is targeted to recruit ecosystem support of the new product.

- The business development strategy may vary depending on the business outcome you are trying to accomplish.

CHAPTER 12

LAUNCH TIME: MARKETING

Launching a new product is an exciting time for the company. Before presenting your product to the market, however, there are a few things you need to do to prepare for the big day.[1] This chapter walks you through before and after the launch as well as ways to assure a successful launch. Among other tried-and-true marketing techniques, you'll learn about recruiting industry influencers, planning leaks of your new product or service, briefing industry analysts and the media, and involving partners.

Essential to a successful product launch is the development of a well-planned marketing campaign. Using a mix of marketing tools is more likely to result in a successful launch. Develop a multifaceted approach to reaching both your existing and your potential customer base that combines traditional advertising, public relations, industry events, social media, website, search engine optimization (SEO), and the sales channels at your disposal to generate a wide range of interest in your product. Neither one of these tools guarantees success, but the more marketing tools you exercise, the better probability of success you will have.

In the old days, there were a handful of publications for each industry. The new media landscape incorporates far fewer major outlets; rather, it is made up of a large number of slimmed-down, focused publications and an inordinate number of specialist bloggers. Getting coverage might be easy, but getting readers' attention is a different story. News releases are coming out at such a high rate that stories are likely to be missed because there is new breaking news just behind it. Innovative tactics are required to get your product or service the notice you want.

Start early. As the title of this book suggests, start selling the chicken soup right after you lay the egg. Get a head start and begin preparing long before you plan to launch. Initiate your outreach activities six to eight weeks before the official launch date and then keep the news going up to, and beyond, that date. Complex campaigns require even more preparation time than do smaller-scale ones. Many industry-specific media outlets have an editorial schedule that focuses on specific topics at prescribed times. By riding on that wave of editorial calendars, it is more likely that you (and your product) will be included in the feature or story that is relevant to your product or service.

Before the Launch

Launching a new product or service is a highly detailed process in which the various activities must be carefully synchronized. It is a good idea to assign a "launch champion" who will serve as a project manager to coordinate and synchronize all the activities that must take place in a precise order and time frame. This section describes some of these activities. It is not mandatory to do them all, but the more the better. Many communication channels lead to the customers' eyes and ears. As there are almost too many these days, it is hard to predict which blog each individual will read and on what date. Thus, the more seeds you throw into the communication maze, the better your chances are that news of your innovation will reach the desired destination—the customer.

Leverage the Power of Industry Influencers and Celebrities

Make the product or service available to important influencers as a first step. Influencers can be friendly customers, celebrities, industry leaders, or even bloggers with a sizable online audience. Encourage these people to use your innovation and then either write their review articles or posts or talk about your products.

Sylvan Goldman did just that—nearly a century ago.

Goldman was the owner of two Piggly Wiggly grocery stores in Oklahoma in the 1920s and 30s. At the time, self-serve grocery stores (including Goldman's) provided customers with only small wire-woven baskets to put groceries in. "When the shopper got her basket full, it was too heavy to carry and she stopped shopping," Goldman recalled in a 1970 interview. "I thought if there was some way we could give the customer two baskets to shop with and still have one hand free to shop, we could do considerably more business."[2]

One evening, Goldman inadvertently locked eyes on a folding chair. An earth-shattering idea took hold: "What if a basket was placed on top of each seat? What if it had wheels?" he said to himself. Shopping cart version 1.0 was invented.

Goldman filed his original patents in 1938. In a later patented model, he replaced the wooden base with a metal one for additional strength.

On June 4, 1936, Goldman constructed a dozen of these rudimentary carts and placed them at the entryway of his Piggly Wiggly stores. The customers were totally unimpressed. "I went into our largest store, and there wasn't a soul using a basket carrier cart. Most of the housewives decided, 'No more carts for me. I have been pushing enough baby carriages. I don't want to push anymore.' The men said, 'You mean with my big strong arms I can't carry a darn little basket like that?' And they wouldn't touch it. It was a complete flop."

A voracious promoter, Goldman rose to the challenge. First, he ran a series of local newspaper advertisements. "It's new. It's sensational. No more baskets to carry!" read one, with an accompanying image of a woman laboriously toting a food-stuffed basket. "Can you imagine," beckoned another, "winding your way through a spacious food market without having to carry a cumbersome shopping basket on your arm?"

When these ads didn't work, Goldman turned to an age-old marketing trick: He hired an attractive girl to stand by the front of the store, offering the carts to shoppers as they walked in. Still, this did little to garner interest. The shopping cart—or the "folding basket carrier," as he called it—just wasn't sexy enough.

Finally, Goldman hired a team of good-looking actors, both men and women, to push the carts throughout his stores, pretending to be customers, picking items off shelves with ease, and wearing beaming smiles as they did so. Before long, herd mentality took hold and shoppers gradually began to accept and cherish the cart.

Once his stores were thriving with happy cart pushers, Goldman filmed his success and showed it to other grocers. Soon, the carts were in high demand: Goldman sold them for $7.00 each and quickly had two years' worth on back order.

Ultimately, his grand plan worked. With the increase in carrying capacity the carts provided, shoppers drastically increased the quantity of their purchases. Goldman's Piggly Wiggly franchise locations thrived, and he amassed a fortune.

Plan Leaks

Another prelaunch technique that generates interest and anticipation is to seed the media space with "leaks." For example, "coming soon" tweets and "leaked" photos of your product create an aura of intrigue that builds interest. Target people who are naturally eager to learn about your offering. Apple is a master of this technique. Way too often before a new iPhone is to launch, some "absentminded" Apple employee leaves behind a new secret unannounced iPhone at some Silicon Valley bar. Too many of these cases have happened to be a coincidence. Chevrolet is also notorious for letting some of their employees drive around in the next-generation Corvette model, which has been partially covered to hide its complete new look but reveals enough to get Corvette enthusiasts fired up.

Inventor and entrepreneur Dean Kamen rolled out his first human transport product, the Segway HT, soon after we crossed into the new century. The original intent for this type of scooter was to provide alternative transportation for short distances in such places as downtown areas in big cities, university campuses, parks, sightseeing venues, and so on.

The Segway HT attracted a lot of attention even before its launch. Steve Jobs was quoted prelaunch as saying that "cities will be built around it." The hype—driven by controlled leaks—was engineered by Kamen himself. Essentially, he wanted to keep his product a secret but, at the same time, let the world know that he was keeping a secret.[3]

The start-up officially announced the launch of the Segway HT on the popular TV show *Good Morning America* in December 2001. Initially, the company was to sell Segway HTs only to commercial establishments. The company targeted large-scale manufacturing plants, warehousing operations, companies in the travel and tourism sector, universities, and the postal service. The company also announced that the Manchester and Boston police departments would be testing its Segway HTs for their practicality in community policing.

The company had expected to sell between 50,000 and 100,000 Segway HTs in the first year of its launch. Instead, it managed to sell a paltry 6,000 in the twenty-one months after the launch. Even in 2004, the company could not sell more than 10,000 units.

In this, Segway is a good example of how challenging the launch of a new product category can be—despite the smart use of marketing activities.[4] Many critics attributed Segway HT's poor sales performance to how the product was marketed and sold. Marketing experts felt that the company made a mistake in not identifying its target audience. By describing the Segway HT as a product for everyone, it diluted the effectiveness of its campaign. Moreover, the initial asking price of US $4,950 was way beyond the reach of most people. (Before the product's launch, it was believed that the price of the Segway HT would be around $2,000.) In addition to the affordability issues, there were questions circling safety and regulatory issues: Is it a motor vehicle? Can it go on the road? On the sidewalk? Other questions concerned infrastructure readiness: Can you load it on a bus? Where do you park it? Will there be public recharging stations? And the list went on and on.

Remember my cautionary note in the introduction to *Lay an Egg and Make Chicken Soup*? Segway did a good job with a few ingredients, but it failed with other ingredients. The result was that the "dish" was not as "tasty" (i.e., successful) as they hoped it would be.

Cue Industry Analysts and the Media

Brief industry analysts during the prelaunch phase as well. Scheduling calls with these folks takes time, so do this early. Invest the time in writing compelling requests for a meeting as well as your talking points. These people are busy, so you will want to make sure your meeting request clearly states why it is worth their time to hear about your company's newest offering.

Keep the press releases rolling. You don't know when reporters will have time to write, so give them some opportunity to write about the offering both before and after the official launch date. Continue to produce fresh newslike announcements concerning novel uses of the product, customer stories, details about how the offering provides return on investment to customers, or photos of your product being used by a celebrity. Talk to reporters about their upcoming stories. Maybe your new product could fit an upcoming article from an alternative angle than what you intended with your straightforward announcement.

For example, during my tenure as CEO of an Israeli technology start-up, we kept our U.S. headquarters in Austin, Texas. When the time came to start briefing the technology media, we asked to meet the technology editor of the local newspaper, the *Austin American-Statesmen*. We thought that as a local Austin start-up, we might get a little coverage and therefore reach potential Austin customers such as Dell and IBM. At the time, there were only three employees in Austin, and we all were traveling so much of the time that we decided not to rent an office. Each one of us worked from home while in town. My "home office" was at a neighborhood Starbucks in the West Lake area of Austin, Texas.

Starbucks was one of the first coffee shops to offer free Wi-Fi, which was a pretty novel workstyle in those days just at the turn of the century. The *Statesmen's* technology editor asked to conduct the interview in "my office," and I gladly invited him to meet me in my Starbucks office. We started to talk about our company and the new technology we were introducing, but very quickly he became interested in the idea that I managed an Israeli start-up, 7,000 miles away, from a Starbucks coffee shop in Austin, Texas. He was so excited about the concept that he made it the cover story for that week's issue.

This is an example of how a different angle can bring you better coverage. In our case, this was much better coverage than we would have gotten had the reporter treated our story as just another product announcement blip. Today, working in a coffee shop is business as usual. Back in 2005, it made the front page!

Get Partners Involved

Channel and marketing partners who have a financial stake in the success of the launch are natural allies. The more people that are talking about the release, the better the chances it will get picked up. In a B2C situation, a partner might be the retail chains that carry the products. Have them do some joint promotional campaign around your new product. In a B2B situation, your product is part of your customer's new product. In such a situation, joint campaigning might work well.

One company that uses joint marketing campaigns effectively is W. L. Gore and Associates, producers of Gore-Tex. Invented in 1969, Gore-Tex is a breathable fabric membrane able to repel liquid water while allowing water vapor to pass through it. It is a lightweight, waterproof fabric for all-weather use. W. L. Gore and Associates has licensed their Gore-Tex technology to numerous other companies to be used in their products (Patagonia's award-winning gear and clothing or Ecco's men's and women's shoes, for example) and have been highly effective in the co-marketing of those products.

Be Boldly Creative

If you truly want to launch your product into the marketplace with a bang, think outside the box. The more creative the better. Think in terms of something that will make people ask their friends and coworkers, "Did you see that great new commercial for . . . ?" Generate that same type of hype about your product launch by maximizing your marketing materials' appeal through creativity.

During the lead-in time to the product launch, release

videos or commercials that are unique in nature or that make people laugh.

Take a poll of your target audience and correlate the responses into an infographic or survey response that lets potential customers see the need for your product.

Consider an industry-related release campaign to capitalize on the days leading up to your launch.

Leverage People with a Vested Interest

Distribute products to the investors who have committed funds to the new product. Let them use the product and begin to tell others about it. By having a vested interest in the success of the product, they will be highly motivated to promote the product among their circle of influence. Using investors to promote the product is a win-win: The product gets attention and generates excitement, and the investors are helping to ensure that they get a higher ROI.

Harness the Power of Social Media

Harness the power of social media by using its numerous channels to generate conversations about the product launch. Explore connections that may exist solely in an online capacity, and develop meaningful interactions with new social circles that may be interested in your product. Instead of focusing on social media numbers, focus on the depth of the interactions you can generate. People are more likely to respond to a recommendation from a trusted friend than by an actor in a TV ad. Provide appealing content about your product and then ignite conversations around it. As the social circle widens and expands, more and more people will begin to talk about the product; these folks will then, in turn, tell others, and on it goes, starting a grassroots movement to spread the word far and wide about your campaign.

Release Your Product or Service

Your launch date has arrived, and you'll soon reap the bounty of all those prelaunch activities. Some of them will also continue during the actual launch. For example, continue to keep the media informed by staging something unusual during the release cycle. Create a funny video, do a stunt centered around an industry event, publish a survey that supports the value of your product, or design an interesting infographic that describes the need for your product.

Here are still more ways to maintain the buzz around your latest product or service.

Target Early Adopters

Some people and businesses are natural early adopters. In the case of consumer products, early adopters want to be the first to acquire a new gadget and become trend setters. (This key motivator is seen mostly with emotionally driven products.) It puts them at the center of attention because they own the latest and greatest gadget to brag about with their friends and family. The other motivator that drives consumers to be early adopters is pure curiosity. Business customers will view being early adopters as a competitive advantage over their competitors, a way to offer better service to their customers, and/or a cost reduction for themselves. Whatever the customers' motivation, your initial marketing efforts should target these early adopter and leverage them later as real-life examples of end users who are enjoying the benefits of your products.

Budget for Giveaways

Do not expect people to spend money on your new product on day one. Most of the time, you will need to lure people to be your early adopters. If your product is so new that customers are not sure if it is worth spending money on it or how much to spend, offer it at a deep discount or seed the market with free samples.

In the case of start-ups, you will have significant pressure from your board of directors to charge full price from day one. Understand that the board is motivated to do so mainly for two reasons: One, as investors in the company, they want to make sure that the market is willing to pay the price you want for your product, and there is no better test than to actually try it. Two, pure greed. This group of stakeholders in particular wants to see revenue and profits as soon as possible, often unknowingly sacrificing the long-term success of the company. The way to justify these lower early prices is either by allocating it to your marketing budget as a promotional cost and/or allocating it to your R&D budget. (Justification: the R&D job is not finished until the new product has reached its cost target.)

Early production batches are likely to cost you more because of learning curve issues. Do not try to price your products based on your early cost structure. Instead, price your product based on what's accepted in the market. If your long-term cost is not low enough relative to your market price, you need to address your production cost or forget about this product altogether. (See chapter 16, "Learning Curve Management," which details the many learning curve issues to consider.)

User Manual

Creating a user's manual is an integral part of any product, especially a complex one. By the time of the launch, the creator of the product is so familiar with it, everything about it feels trivial and a no-brainer. Don't make that mistake. Test the manual with a sample of people unfamiliar with the product. Make your sample group diverse in age, gender, and education to represent the wide variety of potential users. Having read the user's manual, they should be able to get their arms around how to use the product with no help. A poorly conceived and worded manual will result in customer frustration and can easily kill an otherwise good product.

Website

A website is a standard tool that every business needs, whether you are a brick-and-mortar company or an e-commerce one. This is the first place customers normally stop to learn about your business and products. One of the challenges this presents when you're introducing a new product—especially if it's a brand-new product category—is the fact that customers don't know about it. Consequently, they will not know to look for it online. Sophisticated SEO is needed to guide customers to your website, even if they are not specifically searching for that new product.

Provide Adequate Support for the Product or Service

Any new product is likely to trigger questions from prospective buyers. Make sure you have adequate support the day of the launch—and even before. Build a frequently asked questions (FAQs) document over time so the support team can learn how to answer difficult questions. As was an issue with the user's manual, quality communication is essential regarding FAQs. If potential customers or current customers have to wait a long time for answers to their questions they can grow frustrated about the product, which will impact its success long term. That's a real possibility in light of today's social media; any product frustration could go viral and damage your prospects beyond repair.

Addict Customers to Your Product

Get customers addicted to your product. In his best seller *Hooked: How to Build Habit-Forming Products*, author and behavioral designer Nir Eyal offers a four-stage process to get customers addicted, which I've paraphrased below.[5]

> **Step One—Trigger.** Send an email, perhaps, or a direct mail advertisement. It's best if you can make it an invitation from a friend.

> **Step Two—Action.** Motivate them to do something simple with the product.

> **Step Three—Reward.** Once a user completes the action, reward him or her to reinforce the action.

Step Four—Investment. Repeat the motivation step. By asking the customers to do something additional or more advanced with the product, you increase the odds that they will be engaged by this hook cycle model with future products too.

This model works both with B2C products as well as with B2B products. We used a very similar strategy at Motorola whenever we were marketing technology products to engineers. When introducing B2B products to engineers, we always emphasized how the new product would make their life easier by facilitating a better outcome from the engineering tasks they performed. We asked them to do a simple exercise with our new product, and we always offered a small reward to all participants, with an additional, bigger reward based on the homework they contributed. The first prize in one of these new product promotions, for example, was a Corvette. Who could resist that?

Stay Positive and Stay Active

Unless your company is one of the massive industry celebrity organizations dominating the marketplace, your product launch may not even surface on the radar of the mainstream media. This is why you need to implement multiple communication strategies, not knowing in advance which one, or ones, will pick up news of your product launch and run with it. Also try to create some newsworthy angle around the product launch. Media is driven by ratings. They will pick up your story only if they believe it will contribute to more reader hits for them. This rating-stimulation angle may not be a direct fit for your product, but it will provide you with exposure if your product relates to some other interesting news story.

After the Launch

Once the launch date has passed, your efforts should not stop. Your launch promotion must continue.

Maintain a steady supply of topics about the product itself to reporters/journalists.

Detail customer uses of the product, including reports from some of the initial users of the product.

Describe the changes that the product brings to the market.

Keep journalists informed about the product through well-written content articles because they are under significant time constraints and deadlines. If you ghostwrite the material for them, it will increase the chances that they will pick it up.

Throughout the course of the marketing strategy, your campaign will need to be altered as ads become stale, sales become stagnant, or customers seem to lose interest in the product. Be vigilant about keeping track of what efforts are starting to lose effectiveness so that you can make the appropriate changes. Monitoring the market conditions can also be an indicator of when a product has run its course and needs to either be revamped or pulled from the market completely.

In the same manner, keeping track of which media tools were the most successful in converting potential customers into sales will give an indicator of where your efforts and marketing money should be spent. Dropping the ineffectual methods and replacing them with renewed efforts in the productive methods will not only help generate income by identifying new customers; it will maximize the customer awareness.

Marketing and sales departments within a business are paired as often as nachos and cerveza are at parties. So, turn the page for advice on what the sales team needs to focus on when new products or services have been launched.

Takeaways

- Start preparations early.
- Use multiple communication channels.
- Find or create newsworthy stories around your product.
- Focus initially on early adopters and motivate them to try the product. Prepare thorough documentation and support logistics from each product launch to optimize your marketing efforts for future products or services.

CHAPTER 13

SALES

Here's the situation in most sales divisions in the corporate world. Your salespeople are extremely familiar with your existing products and have a good track record selling them. The bread-and-butter products are relatively easy to sell with a predictable commission as a reward. It doesn't take much to refill a purchase order (PO), and even a new flavor of an existing product category does not require a major effort.

When you introduce new products, however, that will slow down the salesperson's productivity; thus, training is required to accelerate that knowledge acquisition. Remember, salespeople are highly driven by commission. Time in the classroom is commission-less. Even when the company is well established, with healthy ongoing business, it's difficult to get salespeople to devote time on new products unless they're properly motivated. One way to motivate them to participate in the training is to offer some additional incentive. This could be as simple as having lunch served in the classroom, door prizes, a cash reward for finishing the test, and so on.

Make sure that the sales training program for each innovative product or service includes the following key points:

1. Know all the reasons why customers need this new product and argue them persuasively.
2. Know how to quickly identify early adopters of the product and reach out to them.
3. Know which of the competition's products are similar and how to sell against arguments in their favor.

Especially if you're a CEO or general manager who didn't come out of a sales background, have a look at the following sections that compare the objectives and motivators of salespeople who sell a business's core product lines and those who specialize in new products.

Conventional Salespeople

Conventional salespeople are used to selling existing products to repeat customers and/or those that already know about the product and its benefits.

The end goal of a salesperson's job is to get a PO. Achieving that for existing products involves a pretty straightforward process. The three growth opportunities in mature products might be the following:

1. Get the customers to use more products.

2. Upsell the product, which means get the customers to buy a higher-end, more expensive version of the product.

3. Get the customers to prefer your company's product to your competitor's.

Note, however, that these three growth opportunities are not always applicable. For example, if a person already has a car it is unlikely that he will buy more cars, in which case option 1 is not relevant. Or, in the case of option 2, if I have already decided to buy the highest-priced package for a Toyota model, there is not much up-sell you can do.

The ecosystem to support this process is assumed to exist. This is also true for a new product that is just a different version or a migration from an existing products' category.

The salespeople are your eyes and ears when it comes to knowing the customers. In this regard they serve the highly important role of listening to customer input about new product needs and communicating that information to the appropriate people in the head office. When I was product planning manager for one of a Motorola's business units, for instance, I formed a product planning committee stuffed full of sales engineers that met in person four times per year with monthly conference calls in between to discuss new product input from customers. We kicked off fifty new products in three years, which fueled the growth from $300 million revenue to more than $2 billion. Some of these new products were enabling technologies for applications that were emerging at the time, such as the first handheld devices (which later became smart phones), computer games, and early versions of smart vehicle applications, to name a few.

New Products Salespeople

When the context is new products, especially new concept products, the sales effort is more time-consuming and multi-dimensional. It takes significantly longer no matter how attractive and exciting the new product is. In fact, the more thrilling and revolutionary the new product is, the longer it may take to diffuse it into the market and the more challenging surviving the Valley of Death becomes for start-ups awaiting cash flow from sales. (See more about this dreaded valley in chapter 11, "Business Development.")

It takes a special kind of salesperson to promote new products. These folks must enjoy the adrenaline rash in the process. Second, they must know the customers well enough to be able to distill a short list of likely innovators and early adopters. Third, they must be very familiar with the decision-making process of each customer, which individuals in the customer's organization are likely to like the product and which ones will try to oppose it, and why. Know your customer exceedingly well—their needs, goals, mission, risk tolerance, and status in the market, among many other details—is sales rule #1. It is particularly crucial in the case of promoting new products.

The implied assumption here is that the new product sales process is primarily used in a B2B situation. But even in the case of B2C products, often the first selling front is the retailer, which needs to decide if and when they want to stock this new product, and what the initial quantities to stock will be.

In my experience, to obtain the highest productivity from this segment of the sales force, the management should offer certain rewards and monetary incentives. Each of these categories is described in the subsections that follow.

Incentives for New Products Salespeople

As I mentioned earlier in this chapter, compensation for salespeople is highly commission based, and very often a commission-only reward structure. This commission arrangement will not work well for compensating new products salespeople, however. That's because they might starve before they could cross the chasm, especially in the case of complex products where the gap between launch and meaningful revenue could be years. Furthermore, even after the chasm is crossed, the sales ramp to high volume is not immediate.

So, additional motivational tools must be added to the mix to attract these salespeople, to entice them to invest their talents fully in selling the new products and to reward them accordingly.

What follows is a list of a few ideas for these incentives to motivate, reward, and retain a high-performing sales team for your company's new innovative products or services. These incentives are relevant both for in-house salespeople and for third-party sales reps and distributors. Some sales channel firms may limit what additional incentives a supplier is allowed to provide. It's prudent to plan the new product launch campaign with the management of your sales channel partners so the additional incentive package will comply with their company's policies— and thus be blessed by the management.

Bonuses for Completing Milestones

Define important milestones for the new product launch and establish a bonus formula based on achieving those. For example, a bonus might be given for taking the new product training and

passing a test. Or a bonus might be offered for signing up customers to attend a class about the new product. Or a bonus might
be given when a customer orders samples of the new product or
upon receipt of the customer's first repeat order.

Increased Commission

Define a launch period during which any sales of the new product will pay a significantly higher commission or margin than
from the sale of mature products.

Exclusivity or Increased Margin

When you have more than one third-party channel partner in
a given territory, they often compete against each other in selling your products. One way to incentivize them to promote a
new product is to grant them exclusivity or an increased margin
for any customer they acquire for the new product. In doing so,
you motivate them to make the initial investment in promoting
the new product knowing that they have the upper hand when
competing with other channel partners on this product once
it is matures into high volume. This kind of incentive process
requires that a system be in place to track and manage the linkage between channel partners, products, and customers for the
proper increased incentives or exclusivity.

Retainer or Base Salary

Pay a base salary to in-house salespeople (or a retainer to third-
party channel partners) with the understanding that this money

is paid to get them across the chasm. This must be documented in the job description, and make sure to clearly define the expectations required for time allocation and expected results in promoting new product launches.

The Selling Process

A product can be sold via in-house sales teams, dealers, reps, distributors, retailers, value-add resellers, e-commerce, or any combination of the above. No matter the sales channel, though, the selling process has but two components: First, knowledge of the product, and second, relationships with the customers.

Let's break down the pros and cons of each of the two main sales channels—direct versus indirect—as well as how to balance a combination of the two approaches for your sales strategy.

Finding the right mix between direct and indirect sales channels depends on the product or service you are offering, the maturity level of the product (for the sake of our discussion, new products), as well as the capabilities and reach of your in-house sales force.

Direct Sales Channels

Direct sales come from selling directly to the end customers using your own in-house sales force or e-commerce vehicles or a combination of the two. A direct sales model requires building and managing a sales team. The sales team needs to be close to your target markets, so if you plan to sell in multiple regions, you will likely need several local sales teams and/or frequent long distance traveling sales force, which may add more costs and management overhead.

Pros for New Product Launch

Knowledge: New product selling requires intimate knowledge of the product and the headquarters resources to support the process.

No channel discounts: Selling directly means that you don't have to share the profit with a reseller or channel partner.

Cons for New Products

High cost: Developing and managing a sales team is expensive.

Difficult to scale: Scaling a sales team requires recruiting, training, and onboarding new salespeople. If you're a smaller company, you may not have the resources to build and manage a significant in-house sales team, especially if you target multiple markets.

Indirect Sales Channels

Selling your product or service through a network of third-party channel partners can provide your business with great leverage. The value that these third parties bring to the table is the reach and relationships with the target customers. Contrast that with your company, especially if it is a start-up, which has limited bandwidth and resources.

Pros for New Product Launch

Relationships: The third-party channel partner usually has an established presence and relationships with the customers. You can reach new customers at a very low initial cost and enter new regions and markets in a cost-effective way.

Effective scaling: If you have an established channel model you can scale very effectively by adding more channel partners into that mix. Every additional channel partner gets you immediate access to numerous new customers.

Start-ups: Early-stage start-ups cannot afford to hire a direct sales team of significant size. Initially, all the start-up can normally afford is a single VP of sales to manage the third-party sales channels.

Bundling and cross-selling: A third-party salesperson often represents several vendors and can benefit you by bundling several synergistic products into the deal.

Cons for New Products

Products knowledge: Selling new products requires a higher level of familiarity with the product, with the company that produced it, and with that company's (the supplier's) in-house resources. This is not a one-size-fits-all selling process, but rather a more sophisticated one that requires significant time holding the hand of the customer as well as coordination with the supplier.

Partner discounts: Depending on the type of partners and the value they provide, you will need to share between 20 percent and 50 percent of your revenues with the partner that makes the sale.

Types of Indirect Sales Channels

There are several different types of indirect, or third-party, sales channel structures: sales reps, distributors, and value-added distributor or system integrator channel partners. Here's a quick description of each that allows you to compare their similarities and differences.

Sales Reps

Sales reps are sales professionals who represent your brand to buyers. They make the introductions, answer initial product questions, help close the sale, and offer post-sale support. That support might come in the form of helping merchandise your products in-store, keeping buyers aware of new product launches and promotions, and passing on product feedback to the maker. Reps' compensation for selling your existing products is commission based. For selling new products, it is customary to add some retainer to the equation to compensate the rep for investing in background work that will not generate short-term sales. See the list of other incentives in the new product salespeople section for other tools to motivate these reps.

e-commerce

A definite special sales channel category is e-commerce (online sales), which is a standard way of doing business for any product nowadays. (See the box titled "e-commerce Model" in chapter 7 for a discussion of e-commerce in the context of business development models.) Though it doesn't require human salespeople, it does require additional marketing techniques to direct customers to your website (or whatever third-party website you post your products on, such as Amazon or Alibaba).

Online shopping offers customers several advantages: the convenience of shopping without leaving your home, a larger selection, and reviews of products from other end users. As the supplier of the product, you need to have the infrastructure to support selling through this channel, such as a virtual shopping cart and the shipping logistics. When it comes to your new product, potential customers may not be aware that it exists, and so they will not look for it. That being so, you may require additional investment in search engine optimization, website design, and online advertising to make sure that your URL appears on the first page of search results so virtual shoppers will click the appropriate link to find your latest offering(s).

Distributors

Distributors are companies that purchase products and inventory before reselling them to end customers. They employ their own salespeople. The distributor makes its money by reselling the products for a profit. For a start-up organization in particular, the fact that a distributor buys the products puts some money in your pocket, and it provides a vote of confidence by an outsider that validates to investors that the company's products are sales worthy.

Simple consumer products are handled by two levels of distributors: the wholesale distributor and the retail distributor. In the case of new products, you need to get the buy-in from both to guarantee your product a spot on the retail shelf.

Some distributors are huge organizations and will not sign up a small start-up. Therefore, a small start-up has a better chance working initially with reps or small niche distributors rather than trying to work directly with the behemoths.

Value-Added Distributor or System Integrator

Sophisticated products often need to be integrated with other components or services to provide a full solution to the end customer.

For example, a small or medium-size business that needs to set up its IT system will hire an IT service provider. The IT service provider will purchase the computers, printers, WiFi routers, accounting software, scheduling software, and purchasing software from different vendors, and then they will integrate them in that business's office. These system integrators buy all the components at wholesale prices, and they sell those components (or lease them) for a profit to cover their work; sometimes, they also add hourly charges on top of that. If your new product is a new type of WiFi router, for example, you need to sell it to the value-added channel of system integrators rather than to the end customer (i.e., the business owner).

Finding the right sales channel or mix of channels often takes time and experimentation. Different territories may require different approaches for the same product or service. Also, it is likely that some channels will be more or less effective at different stages of the evolution of your company and its products. Some channels are doing better at high-volume cookie-cutter sales, while others are more sophisticated and capable in developing new products' business.

Early-stage start-ups may face difficulties in getting established third-party sales channels to accept them as a partner. Part of the business development efforts must go into recruiting channel partners.

Large companies normally have a direct sales in-house team that serves strategic customers and commissions channel partners to handle their smaller customers. Different companies have different policies regarding which customers are served directly versus which ones are asked to buy through the third-party channels.

The supplier should never compete against the third-party channel sales partners it signs on. Some greedy in-house salespeople may attempt to steal customers away from channel partners. *This is a big NO-NO!*

Coordinating Marketing and Sales Efforts

I covered marketing in length in chapter 12, but I want to add a few more words here about coordinating between marketing and sales. The marketing side is called "pull" because it is intended to pull customers toward the new product. The increased sales incentives are called "push" because they encourage the salespeople to push the new product out into the marketplace. An effective new product campaign must create a synchronized "pull-push" to have the maximum impact. Here's what a synchronized pull-push campaign might look like: an aggressive marketing communication campaign (such as ads and press releases to the media) combined with offering early adopters a rebate or a deep discount during that period. At the same time, the new product supplier should implement additional sales incentives to the direct in-house sales force and indirect sales channel partners that are assigned to promote the new product.

Takeaways

- Salespeople are the front line to the customers. Encourage them to communicate new product ideas and customer feedback to the company's innovation team.

- The sales force assigned to sell your new products responds to different motivators and incentives than your more conventional salespeople do.

- e-commerce may bypass some of the obstacles inherent in other third-party sales channels, but it is likely to require additional marketing investments because of the public's lack of awareness of your new product.

CHAPTER 14

SYNCHRONIZE ALL
THE MOVING PARTS

As Microsoft demonstrated with its belated Office 2007 software package and Vista operating system, postponing new product launches can take a heavy toll on the bottom line. The company lost 10 percent of expected sales from June to December 2006 because of these delays.

In the pharmaceutical industry, product life cycles are longer than in high-tech industries. Nevertheless, delays in product introductions shorten the period of exclusivity granted under patent protection. In the meantime, doctors start prescribing other drugs.

Exclusivity regulations vary for different industries and different types of products with complexities beyond the scope of this section.

As these two examples reveal concretely, introduction delays can have a number of negative consequences on revenue. In a competitive industry, customers may not be willing to wait, choosing to buy a competitor's product instead of yours. When product life cycles are short, delays reduce the window of opportunity to generate revenues. Postponing can also cause the product to become obsolete faster. Deferral of introduction is also likely to negatively impact the bottom line as it reduces the premium margin companies often take when competition is not so intense. Regarding seasonal products, such as products targeted for Christmas, by not making it on time for delivery before the holidays, the company may lose a whole year.

Studies confirm that reality. For example, management science professors Vinod Singhal and Kevin Hendricks analyzed the financial performance of a diverse set of 450-plus publicly traded firms that experienced product introduction delays between 1987 and 2003. In their study, the researchers used operating income to measure profitability. Examining operating performance both before and after product delay announcements, the researchers found that the mean decline in return on assets was roughly 6.9 percent over a three-year period following the year in which the delay announcement was made.[1]

Don't despair, however. Overpromising and underdelivering doesn't have to be in your business's future. In the following sections, I spell out the areas in product development that could potentially result in delays and then show you how you can mitigate the risk of such delays.

New Product Launch Risks

Here it is in a nutshell: The biggest challenge your innovation team faces in managing launch timing is that it depends on so many parameters being ready simultaneously, and the timing of the introduction will be determined by the slowest ingredient in the launch mix.

Let's take a closer look at the most common risk factors in new product launch.

Launch Campaign Loses Sync

As you're well aware, many components must come together during launch time: Finish the design on time. Complete product testing. Build inventory. Train the sales force. Document each stage of product development. Polish the public relations and advertising campaign. And the list goes on and on. Any delay in one parameter will delay the entire program.

Here are ways to mitigate those timing risks.

- Have all functions and departments involved in the planning process from the beginning because you can't second-guess how long task X or task Y will take.

- All parties involved in the execution must be present in the project review meetings. During the early days of the project, monthly meetings may suffice, and as you get closer to the finish line, the frequency should shift to weekly and even daily meetings.

- Each function must plan its own mitigation and communicate any potential delays ASAP so proper correction can be taken in a timely manner.

My favorite example is from my own product launch experience in the inauguration of a new Motorola product back in the mid-1990s. One of the ingredients in the launch campaign was a textbook written by our staff that was supposed to educate the users about this new technology. As we came closer to kickoff, it became apparent that the textbook would not be ready on time. A draft was in decent shape, but we didn't have sufficient time for a final review and correction cycle. Our options were to delay the whole campaign, drop the textbook from the campaign, or somehow turn the situation to our advantage. Luckily, we found a way to turn this lemon into lemonade.

The recovery plan was to introduce the draft, on time, as is. But we also announced that we would give a $100 reward to every reader who reviewed the draft and submitted his or her comments. This solution worked well on two fronts: It saved the campaign and our face to start with. More importantly, it encouraged our audience to invest the time in reading the book and to draw our attention to faults it in. Out of the 10,000 people who purchased the draft textbook as part of this campaign, only one customer suspected that this was a trick to hide a delay in schedule (and he condemned us for doing that). The moral of the story: The author of the textbook was brave and honest enough to report his delay early on, which allowed us time to change our course of action and to recover. The organizational culture must be one of constructive collective problem-solving rather than one of punishing the slackers.

As part of the launch plan, as with any other project plan, a thorough risk analysis must take place. First, prioritize the must-have ingredients for the launch versus the nice-to-have ones. Next, analyze the risk factors related to each of the items in the plan. Third, design a mitigation plan for each must-have ingredient with a probability of its risk factor occurrence significant enough to worry about.

Perfect timing and coordination are keys to a successful launch.

Reality Different from Forecast

Estimating demand for an existing product is fairly predictable, but forecasting how many units you'll sell of a brand-new product is very difficult because of its lack of history. In chapter 5, "Estimating Demand for a New Product," I talked a lot about reliable forecasting techniques. Here, I am mentioning forecasting again, but in the context of "miss-forecasting," which is a marketing issue as well as an operational one: Marketing are the ones responsible for the forecast, but operations are the ones responsible for the mitigation plan. That is, the focus is risk mitigation in case the reality is different from the forecast, which happens more often than not. The damage to the new venture's success could be that you built too many products, and thus end the campaign with unsold inventory, or that you built too few, which may cause customers to lose interest or turn to alternatives.

Here are several proven techniques you should implement to mitigate forecast risks.

Keep an Inventory of Work in Progress

Build a reasonable number of the product that you are highly confident your team can sell. Build a mitigation batch and keep it "half-baked" at some interim production stage. The benefit here is twofold. One, should demand be surprisingly higher than was forecast, your reaction time will be faster because the backup inventory of half-baked products can be readied in much shorter time to reach the finish line. Two, should demand be lower than expected, the financial consequence is reduced because the cost of making the half-baked products is much lower than the cost would be for finished goods.

Minimize the Options

Having product options complicates the uncertainty of demand even more because you have to guess right about each one of the options. This is a planning nightmare. One of the reasons for the poor execution of the Edsel's launch (which you read about in chapter 5) is the fact that Ford offered seven models. That not only complicated the inventory management, it also complicated the production line, thus causing quality issues. In contrast to the Edsel, Ford's Model-T had no options, not even different colors.[2]

Southwest Airlines (NYSE:LUV) is a good example of a streamlined operation. By choosing only one aircraft model—the Boeing 737—it simplified their maintenance operations and their spare parts inventory management. By deciding to offer no meals, they simplified their ground operations. After all, it's so much simpler to load the airplane with a tray of peanuts than with hundreds of containers of several choices of entrées and desserts. And Southwest's no seat assignment policy accelerates the boarding process.

Shorten Cycle Time

Shorter manufacturing cycle time facilitates faster response to changing conditions. In the case of new product introductions, a shorter cycle time allows you to build a smaller initial inventory and to react more quickly as demand builds up. One of Dell Technologies (NYSE:DVMT) secrets of success is its production cycle time, which is seven days versus eighty days for their closest competitor.[3] They configure their computers with pre-manufactured building blocks, which are held in their suppliers' inventories and pulled from there for final assembly based on orders from the market.

Software Customization

Yes, we are talking about "hardware" products here. Many technology-based hardware products today are being manufactured with their fully loaded configuration. However, the optional features are not activated. This means the optional features are being activated in the field—for example, at the retail shop—with the customer charged different prices depending on the configuration they choose. The benefits derived from the simplicity of offering a single hardware model outweigh the cost savings of having several hardware options in the product. This technique is commonplace in the production of cell phones, computers, and even automobiles. This technique allows you to have different virtual models without complicating the hardware production. Samsung calls it "consumer software customization" (CSC), which they use to show or hide specific features and options in their devices based on geographical region and available mobile carriers.

Pre-Build Platforms

Pre-build generic platforms and design the product to accept customization at the last stage of production. With new products, plan for the platform to include just the standard basics and add the new features further down the line. Similar to the half-baked inventory approach, this will allow you to keep an inventory of generic platforms and be ready to respond to market demand quickly via final configuration. In the construction industry, builders will often pre-build the basic skeleton. After the house is sold, the finishing configuration decided on by the buyer will be implemented.

This same technique is used in fast casual and casual restaurants where they partially prepare basic ingredients to mix and match based on the particular dish their customers choose.

Take Preorders

In the sale of very expensive items such as airplanes and high-end automobiles, taking preorders is business as usual. Taking preorders allow the supplier to build based on actual demand rather than forecast; thus, the inventory risk we discussed before is significantly reduced (theoretically eliminated). But even suppliers with less expensive products than Apple are amenable to accepting preorders.

Early Failure Risks

Yet another new product launch risk is that of the venture's reliability and potential failure.[4]

As you'll see in the graphic later in this section, the reliability life cycle over the life of a product normally takes a bathtub shape: The early failure rate—often referred to in engineering slang as "infant mortalities"—might occur because the design was less than optimal, the production was second rate, or the quality control was insufficient. The middle part of the reliability curve is normally flat, driven by a random evenly distributed failure rate. When approaching its normal end of life, a product will increase its failure rate due to accumulated wear and tear. End-of-life wear and tear is typical only of hardware products. A software product will demonstrate end-of-life type issues in the following cases: The hardware platform the software runs on is experiencing wear and tear. Or the software upgrades grew beyond the capability of the original hardware platform that it runs on. Or an older release that hasn't been updated eventually loses its compatibility with other products it interfaces with.

Even after you have created the most perfect product in the lab or on your drawing board, unexpected problems are likely to occur—at any stage. What to do? Plan for these contingencies. Task team members with being prepared to respond with lightning speed to any product defects, no matter how insignificant, before they become a large problem. Too many failures of a new product could damage the image of the product as well as of your company for a long time.

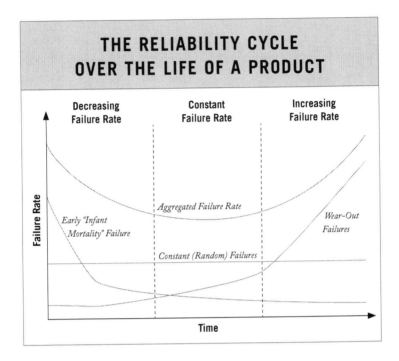

The good news is that there are three effective ways you can address the early failure rate, or infant mortalities.

1. Take a sample of prototypes and stress them beyond their normal use to accelerate the discovery of design marginalities and infant mortality failures. Conducting such tests in the failure analysis lab will enable you to identify the cause(s) of failure and to implement the proper corrective actions. Keep in mind, of course, that stress tests will mean different things to different types of products and services. A software product will go through a different stress test than will a new automobile or a new banking service.

2. Even if you execute the above recommendation, you may want to play it safe and assume that a higher rate of infant mortalities will still exist. Reinforce among members of the support infrastructure in the company that they are to accept returned products, to replace them immediately with new ones, and to send the defective ones to the failure analysis lab. Analysis by the lab staff should be shared with the design team so problems can be addressed and corrective action taken promptly. Call it a fact of life or view it as part of the learning curve: A higher frequency of early failure is expected and is the norm. It's human nature to make mistakes: The design engineer could be responsible for the error (or marginality), or it could occur on the production floor where the manufacturing people are not experienced enough with the new product. In a perfect world, it shouldn't happen, but real life is never perfect.

3. Implement more rigorous product testing and quality control procedures than are normally done for mature products. It is also recommended that staff take samples from each production batch and run them through accelerated stress tests. This will catch production-related variations that contribute to infant mortalities.

This infant mortality issue is part of a product learning curve and adds to the unit cost of early production. (Lessening the occurrence and impacts of the early failure rate is part of the learning curve of every new product. I devote the entire next chapter to managing the learning curve.) An important factor to mention here is that different types of products have correspondingly different sensitivities to failure as expressed by customers in the marketplace. The liability of a new passenger plane crashing is not the same as the sole of a new shoe coming unglued.

Apple's (NASDAQ: AAPL) "Early Field Failure Analysis" (EFFA) team is tasked with identifying problems that early buyers of Apple products might face upon using any given device. The team is then further tasked with ensuring that each one of those problems is eliminated so that they do not "spread" into too many hands. It would pay for you to remember that the maximum number of problems is reported during the initial days of a product launch. Apple knows this for a fact; hence, EFFA is most active whenever Apple launches a new Mac, MacBook, or "iAnything."

Analysis by Apple experts indicates that the majority of problems with Apple devices occur because components have not been connected well, an unconnected cable, improper soldering, and the like. Each hour a problem goes unnoticed or undetected, Apple manufacturers continue to manufacture defective devices at full speed. The result: Thousands of defective phones enter the market, resulting in thousands of unhappy and disappointed customers, and millions of dollars spent in repairing or replacing them. Consequently, the EFFA team is on its toes 24/7 to stanch those negative numbers.

In chapter 17, "Risk Management for New Products," I discuss how to manage risk in much greater depth.

Takeaways

- Many moving parts must come together at launch time. The overall launch schedule will be dictated by the slowest element.

- Delay in launch is likely to lower profitability and open a window of opportunity to competition. Use mitigation techniques to reduce schedule risks.

PART VI

MORE INGREDIENTS FOR THE CHICKEN SOUP

"I think that our fundamental belief is that for us growth is a way of life and we have to grow at all times."

—Mukesh Ambani, chairman, managing director of Reliance Industries Limited

CHAPTER 15

THE HUMAN FACTOR— THE ORGANIZATION

A corporation's approach to organizational structure lies along a spectrum. At one end is the traditional functional, or departmental, organization, where each department has a manager who reports to the CEO or to the general manager of the business unit. The functional organization focuses on discipline specialties.

At the other end of the spectrum is a company organized by product, where each of the managers has a product line responsibility and direct reports from each discipline to contribute to product success. Here the trade-off is project focus versus professional specialty.

Obviously there are "fifty shades" in between these two approaches, collectively called matrix organizations. The CEO has to decide what type of organization best fits the mission and goals of the business he or she runs.

In this section, I have reviewed the pros and cons of a few of these options and their impact on new product success.[1] My focus is primarily on the implications of the organizational structure regarding new products and innovation—conceding that there are other considerations beyond the innovation aspect.

Functional (or Departmental) Organization

A functional organization has a general manager or CEO at the top. Reporting to him or her are different departments, such as engineering, marketing, finance, sales, manufacturing, human resources, and so on, each specializing in one discipline. This functional organization approach offers a business two main advantages:

1. It creates an environment where synergy and cross-training among the different individuals within each department grows and flourishes.

2. It allows company management to deploy people as needed during different phases of the project. Often, the number of people from each department who are required for the new product or service project changes over time. During the development phase, there are more design and R&D people, while few staff are needed from the other departments because the workload isn't sufficient to fill even one person's time. During product maturity phases, however, more people from marketing, sales, and manufacturing are required, and only a skeleton team of R&D and design are there to support any issues that come up after launch.

The main challenge with a functional organization is the difficulty in coordinating the work of the disparate specialties that are often required for the execution of the project. Chief among the hurdles management must clear are incompatibilities in the relationships or interfaces between different parts of the product and the different decision-making processes in each department.

A department manager may have made a change in the work plan or people's priorities, assuming that it won't present a problem to others working on the project, when in fact it does. This failure to communicate or coordinate the work is not necessarily the result of any mean-spiritedness or narrow-mindedness by participants, but rather the result of not seeing other participants regularly and therefore not understanding what they are doing.

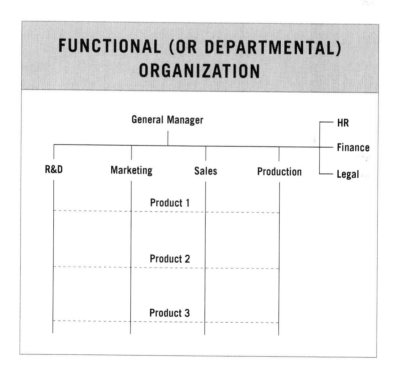

FUNCTIONAL (OR DEPARTMENTAL) ORGANIZATION

Product Line Organization

In a product line–based organization, the focus is always on the project at hand. This type of organization offers a business two main advantages:

1. The ultimate decision maker at the top is the product manager, and her sole priority is the execution on the new product.

2. The product manager has full control of the product budget. Participants in the product's growth phases and launch do not have to fight over resources on a day-to-day basis. Once the budget is allocated to the project, it is the product manager's responsibility to execute on it.

The main disadvantage of this product line–based approach is that some of the resources are not fully utilized all the time. For example, during the early-development days, some of the manufacturing or sales resources are not fully utilized, while during the later phases of the project, some of the engineering resources may be idle. In the departmental structure, the time allocation among individuals is easier to change in real time because they are not dedicated to one product, so a person may spend 70 percent of the time on product A and 30 percent of the time on product B. In a product line–based organization, however, that person is working on the product A team, and her workload requires only 70 percent of the time (same as before), but now she will be idle 30 percent of the time without a product B to work on.

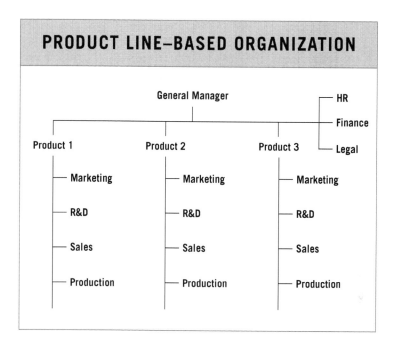

PRODUCT LINE-BASED ORGANIZATION

General Manager

HR
Finance
Legal

Product 1

Product 2

Product 3

- Marketing
- R&D
- Sales
- Production

- Marketing
- R&D
- Sales
- Production

- Marketing
- R&D
- Sales
- Production

The Matrix Organization

Matrix organizations were created to solve the problems inherent in each one of the two organizational structures just described because, in the real world, project managers and department heads often miscommunicate or disagree with one another.

In a pure matrix organization, each employee has practically two supervisors: his functional supervisor and his project supervisor. Once an employee is assigned to a project, the project manager becomes his second, or project, supervisor. The functional supervisor will offer professional guidance, mentorship, and seniority wisdom. The project supervisor calls the shots in regard to time spent on each task and prioritizing between tasks related to the project. The functional supervisor cannot borrow that employee for other tasks unless the project supervisor agrees to it.

In reality, things within a corporation are not so crisply defined, and real life could be even more complicated for the employees. For example, if a certain function is not fully utilized by any one project, an employee may be assigned to several different projects, reporting to the functional supervisor as well as to the several corresponding project managers of those projects. The following illustration shows a marketing person working for both Product 1 and Product 2.

This structure requires good teamwork between the functional managers and the product managers to not confuse the employees with conflicting orders.

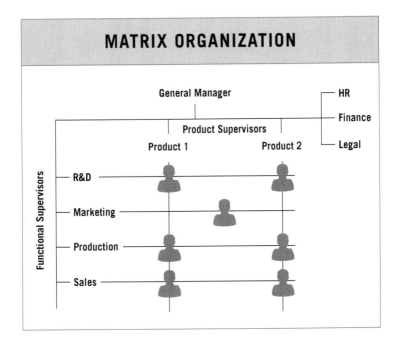

Sometimes, the matrix could become multidimensional, especially in a global company. In addition to reporting to the functional supervisor and the product supervisor, an employee may find herself reporting to the country manager as well. The Airbus A380 case study later in this chapter will show how an overly complicated organization can hamper project execution.

The employees in such a complex organization must learn how to manage the inside politics between the different departments and different managers they have to juggle. (Otherwise, they will not survive.) In these vast multisite organizations, team building becomes significantly more expensive and logistically complex yet even more crucial to the execution of the project. When all the members of the team are working in the same location, the human social integration happens naturally during normal business hours (such as going out for lunch or taking coffee breaks together), and any team-building outings are just icing on the cake. In a multisite situation—especially when those sites span the globe—cementing the human friendships could happen only during the in-person team meetings and team-building getaways.

How Suppliers Should Approach a Complex Organization

Especially when you begin to promote your new product or service among such complex organizations, you must know both the internal politics and the decision-making process within each business.

While I was working for Motorola, for instance, one of the computer-aided design (CAD) vendors spent a whole year trying to sell their solution to the central CAD technology group inside the company, believing that it was the part of the organization empowered to decide which CAD software was best for the entire organization. Little did they know that the charter of that CAD technology group limited them to making recommendations only to the different R&D teams; they couldn't force their preferences on any of the R&D managers, who had the liberty to choose their own tools. When that vendor finally convinced the centralized CAD technology group that their product was the best, they thought that their selling effort was over. They knocked on the doors of the different R&D managers telling them that they must buy their product because it was the chosen one. To their surprise, they did not get the purchase order they were hoping for because the R&D managers had different opinions about what CAD tool was best for their specific needs. Furthermore, the different R&D managers didn't like to be told what CAD tool to use, and they made that vendor's life even more difficult just to teach them a lesson.

The Case of Airbus A380

The Airbus (XETRA: AIR) A380 project is a perfect storm that illustrates the inherent challenges in executing on a complex project in a convoluted matrix organization.[2]

Airbus is an extremely complex organization whose origin comes from mergers between several national aviation agencies in different European countries, each with its own culture and technical specialty. Corporate politics drive them to allocate a fair part to each one of these teams in every project, which complicates the management and execution.

As the world's largest commercial aircraft, the Airbus A380 is a marvelous engineering accomplishment. With two full decks, a wingspan wider than a football field, and space for up to 850 passengers, the A380 is the most complex aircraft of its time. The project that created this behemoth suffered its fair share of problems and delays. Originally scheduled for delivery in 2006, the aircraft's entry into service was delayed by almost two years, and the project was several billion dollars over budget.

At the heart of the problems were difficulties integrating the complex wiring system needed to operate the aircraft with the metal airframe through which the wiring needed to thread. With its 530 kilometers of wires, cables, and wiring harnesses weaving their way throughout the airframe, and with more than 100,000 wires and 40,300 connectors performing 1,150 separate functions, the Airbus A380 has the most complex electrical system the company has ever designed. As the first prototype (code named F-WWOW) was being built in Toulouse, France, engineers began to realize that they had a problem. Wires and their harnesses had been manufactured to specification, but during installation, the wires turned out to be too short.

Internal reviews identified the source of the problem: The different design groups working on the project had used different CAD software to create the engineering drawings. Engineers at sixteen R&D centers across four countries had collaborated in designing and developing the aircraft. German and Spanish designers had used CAD version 4, while British and French teams had already upgraded to CAD version 5. In theory, the electrical system designed in Germany should have been compatible with the airframe components designed in France.

Unfortunately, the construction of the F-WWOW demonstrated that theory and practice are not always the same.

In part, the problem was that the CAD version 5 was not completely compatible with version 4. Calculations used to establish bend radii for wires as they wove through the airframe were inconsistent across the different versions of the software, and that inconsistency resulted in the problem. Stripping out the wiring from the prototype, redesigning the wiring, making new harnesses, and then rethreading the wiring into the airframe took months to complete, and the project was delayed several times.

The root of the problem can be traced back to one decision: the go-ahead to proceed with the project despite the fact that two CAD systems were in use. A lot of background led to that decision. Much of the context had to do with the aerospace pioneer's history being the result of merging national aviation agencies from several European countries. Merging disparate entities into a single homogeneous whole is never easy. Different parts of the organization inherit different corporate cultures, national prides, management styles, and IT systems. Those differences can be both hard and expensive to overcome, and at Airbus, a number of such differences were still deeply entrenched when the A380 project began. The simple matrix organization I described previously is child's play relative to the Airbus corporate structure. Even at the very top of the organization, there were two co-CEOs, one French and one German, which created an elaborate split between France and Germany over control. In 2001, when the A380 program manager attempted to move the German designers onto the same CAD system as the French, he met a firm resistance.

Personal rivalries and national pride are reported to have been issues that stood in the way, and ultimately the pressure to keep the project moving forward meant that the CAD version issue was never resolved.

Eventually F-WWOW did fly, and the aircraft is indeed a wow, but not before the seed of that one small decision point grew to become a billion-dollar delay. Of course, interoperability of design tools is not only an Airbus issue. In today's complex integrated supply chains, stories of failed configuration management during the design process are sadly all too common.

The root of the problem: an overly complex organizational structure that attempted to keep different parts of the organization happy rather than focusing on how best to build the aircraft.

Who Champions the Innovation?

As many organizations have recognized the need for product innovation in order to survive, they have responded by creating a C-level executive position to look after innovation and new products. Some of the common titles given that position are chief technology officer (CTO), chief innovation officer (CNIO), and chief technology innovation officer (CTIO). Some of the individuals in this function are scientists who perceive their roles as chief inventor officer, and their behavior reflects the attitude that once they invent something, they are free to simply throw it over the wall for the rest of the organization to worry about executing. This is the wrong approach. As we have seen throughout this book, product innovation is a multidisciplinary process. The

CTO, CNIO, and CTIO must be the champion of the entire process and not just invent and forget. An invent-and-forget attitude could easily lead to failures because the business discovers that the new invention is not needed, or that the product is not manufacturable, or that, as designed, the product is too expensive, or other real-life issues that must be addressed to guarantee a successful product. Surely the originator of the newborn wants to stay involved in its maturation, right?

A Start-Up's Organizational Structure

Every start-up must have at least three strong skills represented by the management team:

- The first strong skill is to know the market, the customers, the competition, the ecosystem of supporting businesses, and the channels to the markets, which includes having relationships with all of them. The person with this skill usually becomes the VP of marketing, sales, or business development.

- The second important skill is technical know-how, which means the knowledge of how to make the new product or service happen. The person with this ability usually becomes the CTO or the VP of Engineering.

- The third critical skill is the mastery of a business's financial aspects. Every start-up must have a financial model with which to test the basic ROI scenarios. Because this financial function requires very limited time initially, it can usually be performed by a part-time outside service at the start-up's earliest stage.

The initial team is often called the founding team or founders. Often, one of these founders becomes the CEO of the start-up company, at least at the beginning. Initially, the CEO is the one to drive the vision, review it with a few potential customers, put together the business plan, and most importantly, be the main face to the investment community.

Different size companies require different skills from their CEOs. To launch a company successfully, for example, a founder-CEO doesn't necessarily have the skill sets to manage the company as it matures to hundreds of employees with the advent of manufacturing and sales. Sometimes, there comes a point in a company's growth trajectory when a new CEO needs to be hired to lead the company to the next level. This can be a difficult decision to make, but it's better for the founder-CEO to make the decision herself rather than to be told by the board that they're hiring her replacement. Founder-CEOs who have made it through multiple phases of growth are the exception.[3]

When professor Noam Wasserman, author of the best-selling *The Founder's Dilemmas: Anticipating and Avoiding the Pitfalls That Can Sink a Startup*, analyzed 212 American start-ups that sprang up in the late 1990s and early 2000s, he discovered that most founders surrendered management control long before their companies went public. By the time the ventures were three years old, 50 percent of founders were no longer the CEO; in year four, only 40 percent were still in the corner office; and fewer than 25 percent led their companies' initial public offerings.[4] Other researchers have subsequently found similar trends in various industries and in other time periods. A handful of founder-CEOs in the current corporate world come to mind, but they're the exceptions to the rule.

Wasserman coined the term "founder's dilemma" to refer to

this reality, and it has become an industry standard figure of speech (much like chicken and egg).

Another way to refer to it is the rich versus king dilemma. In essence, the founder-CEO must inevitably decide whether to keep his control of the company and risk the possibility that the company will outgrow his skill set to manage it? Or does he bring in an outside CEO more skilled in managing larger operations, thus maximizing the founder's potential financial gain when the company is being acquired or goes public?

THE RICH VERSUS KING DILEMMA

	Limited	Maximum
Limited	Failure	Rich
Complete	King	Exception

CONTROL (vertical axis)

FINANCIAL GAIN (horizontal axis)

I was once hired to be that outside CEO for a start-up, replacing the founder-CEO. During the interview process, I sensed some tension between the founders and the investors. Only after I started my job, and attended the first board meeting, did I realize how bad the situation was. Usually in early-stage start-ups, the founders are represented on the board of directors. In that particular situation, one of the founders' board members preferred to be the king of a financially handicapped company, while the other founders understood the trade-off they had to make and gave away part of their control in order to eventually make more money for themselves later. This caused enormous contention among the founders and between the founders and the investors.

It took me a whole year to repair that ailment. The tricky part in such situations is the fact that the founders are equal board members on the board of directors but also employees of the company in the day-to-day work. Sometimes, the short-term goal of maximizing one's situation as an employee collides with the long-term financial endurance of the company. A person needs a certain level of maturity to make that trade-off for him- or herself.

Takeaways

- In very large companies and with complex projects, a multifaceted matrix organization may evolve. This requires good teamwork among the managers to give the employees coherent marching orders.

- Be careful to not jeopardize the project because of organizational politics. If you sell your new products to a complex organization, make sure you know the inside politics and decision-making process.

- The executives responsible for new product innovation must perceive themselves as championing the *entire* process, not just the inventor of the new product.

- A founder-CEO doesn't always have the skill set to manage the company through its entire growth phases, and often an outside CEO may be required to take over at some point.

CHAPTER 16

LEARNING CURVE MANAGEMENT

A learning curve is a concept that depicts the relationship between cost and output quantities over time. When we're talking about an individual production worker, better means more units per a specified period of time with fewer errors and rejects. This is also true for the entire production facility or enterprise. In a more general sense, the more you repeat a task, the more efficient you become at performing it, whether you are a dentist, a bank teller, or a server at a restaurant.[1]

Background

The learning curve was first described by psychologist Hermann Ebbinghaus in 1885 and is used as a way to measure production efficiency and to forecast costs. In the visual representation of a learning curve, a steeper slope indicates initial learning and translates into higher cost savings; subsequent learning results in cost savings that are increasingly slower and more difficult to obtain.

The learning curve is also referred to as the experience curve, the cost curve, the efficiency curve, or the productivity curve. This is because the learning curve provides measurement and insight into all aspects of a company. The premise underlying the learning curve is that any person, regardless of job or undertaking, takes time to learn how to carry out a specific task or duty. Initially, the amount of time needed to produce the associated output is high. Then, as the task is repeated, the person learns how to complete it quickly and reduces the amount of time needed for a unit of output.

The following chart is the simplest form of a learning curve:

Why is it important to discuss a learning curve when dealing with the introduction of new products in the market? The answer is this: Knowing the slope of your learning curve will allow you to estimate the product cost when it reaches volume production and thereafter use it in your business plan. (Have another quick look at the New Idea Evaluation Checklist in chapter 4.) What I am saying here is that the cost is not static over time; it goes down with volume. This cost reduction needs to be accounted for in the business plan in order to estimate both future profits and future room for price reduction.

People often make the mistake of estimating the cost based on the first few units made. This could kill a good new product because the cost of early units is often much higher than the market will pay.

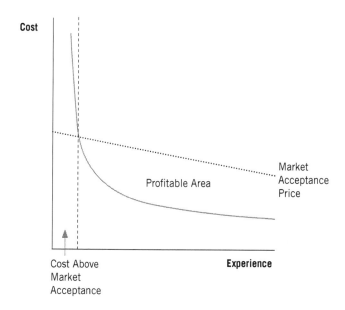

One of my mentors at Motorola, Gary Daniels, used to say, "If you price your product based on your initial manufacturing cost, you will never reach volume production." Why? Because no one will buy those first units, and that means you lack sufficient volume buildup to reach a significant cost reduction in the long run that would allow you to offer the product at a price customers could afford. You need to price the product based on the market acceptance price and push your learning curve aggressively to reach profitability as early as possible. A normal learning curve will happen naturally. If you want to accelerate the learning curve, you have to be a little more proactive. The specific techniques depend on the industry, but one thing is for sure: If you want to drive an initiative, assign a champion for it and empower that champion to lead the task at hand—in this case, cost reduction.

How to Deal with Learning Curve Losses

Now that we understand how the higher cost of early production is not here to stay, how do we deal with the possible loss created by selling early products at market price, which might be lower than our early manufacturing cost? When the cost-price gap is not too high and the slope is reasonably fast, you can allocate these losses to R&D or to marketing.

The justification for an R&D allocation is that the R&D job is not completed until you have figured out a way to build the product in a profitable manner. In other words, the cost reduction of early days is considered part of R&D's responsibility. The justification for a marketing allocation is that it is much like the common practice of acquiring early adopters by giving away free samples. Selling early products at a loss could be considered akin to partially free samples intended for early adopters' acquisition.

When the slope of the learning curve is too long to allow for the previously described accounting allocation, other techniques are needed to keep the business going without losing too much money while fixing learning curve related issues.

Price Sensitivity Segregation

When early production is too expensive to appeal to the general market, a business may decide to introduce the initial models to niche segments that are less cost sensitive than the general audience is. For example, early commercial cell phones were initially introduced in the 1980s to serve business applications that were able to justify the high price in order to stay connected anytime, anywhere. Cell phones became a teenager's commodity only twenty-plus years later.

An even older example is computers. The classic IBM 360 computer was introduced in 1964 and was the first computer built with semiconductors technology. Its most powerful model, the IBM 360–195, ranged in price between $7 million and $12 million, depending on its configuration. Its storage capacity and performance are a joke today compared to any smart phone, game console, or automobile engine computer.[2]

What do you do in such cases where the early cost is extremely high and there's no clear path leading to a significant cost reduction in the near future? Taking that example of IBM's 360 computers, the early adopters were large organizations—governments, financial institutions, NASA, and large universities, among others—that had a justifiable ROI even when factoring in the high sticker price. Smaller businesses and organizations leased computing time and storage space, much like people do today in the cloud (albeit for different reasons). It took almost twenty years for computer technology to become affordable for small businesses and individuals.

Buy versus Lease Business Models

Another technique to make a product that's too expensive more affordable is to implement a business model based on lease or pay-per-use. A common practice today, for instance, is to incorporate the cost of the cell phone into your service contract and pay for it with monthly installments as part of your cell phone bill. A commonplace pay-per-use example is that whenever most of us fly, we "rent" a seat on a commercial flight—because few people own a private airplane. When television sets were too expensive to be in every middle-class home, people used to go to movie theaters to watch a movie—and even to watch the newsreels.

To summarize, the following techniques can be used when the initial production cost is higher than the going market acceptance price:

- If the gap is not too significant, and an acceptable cost reduction is expected in the short term, subsidize the product and allocate the difference to R&D or marketing.
- Lease instead of sell.

- If there's a significant long-term gap, focus on applications and segments that must have the product at all cost, such as governments, medical facilities, or the superrich.

DC-3: A Classic Example of a Government-Paid Learning Curve

The DC-3 is a popular transport aircraft that started its career in the 1930s and served all over the world for many years—in some places even up to now. It is an excellent example of learning curve management at multiple levels.[3] The DC-3 was a larger version of its precursors the DC-1 and DC-2. The DC-1's inaugural flight was on July 1, 1933, followed shortly thereafter by a larger, modified version, the DC-2. The DC-3 was increased in size yet again and first flew on December 17, 1935.

During World War II, the DC-3 (named Dakota by the British) was mass-produced as a utility transport in the C-47, C-53, and other versions—known also as Skytrains and Skytroopers—and was licensed-built in large numbers in Russia as the Lisunou Li-2. Used in all imaginable roles, from freight and personnel transport to glider tug and ambulance, the type was active in all theaters of war, notably during the D-Day landings in Normandy and subsequent assaults by Allied airborne forces.

After the war ended, a huge inventory of used military DC-3s was released to the world, together with thousands of trained pilots and mechanics as well as inventory of spare parts. The many hours the planes had flown during the war contributed to continuous quality improvements of the DC-3, which also contributed to significant improved safety.

The DC-3 overwhelmed the air-travel industry. It was the first plane that could fly from New York to Chicago nonstop, and it made the 700-plus-mile trip in roughly four hours. For comparison, a train trip from New York to Chicago took more than twenty hours. Round-trip, coast-to-coast flights were a pricey $300, the equivalent of roughly $5,000 today, but business customers in particular flocked to take advantage of savings in time. Despite significant cost reductions, flying was still too expensive for most people. Consequently, the service level on these flights was optimized at what we would categorize today as first class.

The DC-3 story demonstrates the learning curve discussion at multiple levels. First, leverage the learning curve paid by the government, which is normally less cost sensitive. Second, if your venture is still too expensive, start by catering to affluent customers that can afford the higher introduction price.

Takeaways

- Product or activity costs decline as more repetitions (i.e., experience) are acquired.

- Expect that your initial product costs may exceed market acceptance price.

- In the case of a short-term learning curve period, subsidize early units and allocate the loss to R&D or marketing.

- If the expected learning curve is too long, initially target niche markets that can accept the higher price and use this experience to drive the cost down.

CHAPTER 17

RISK MANAGEMENT FOR NEW PRODUCTS

A ny business carries some level of uncertainty because it relies on the future. I invest X today hoping to get Y in the future. The X is present, thus deterministic. The Y is a forthcoming event, thus it has a certain level of uncertainty attached to it. Even fairly safe investments—government bonds, for example—are not totally risk free.

When you buy an existing business with a pretty stable history of revenue and profit stream, the future may still bring surprises, some positive, some negative. While positive surprises are always welcome, negative surprises must be mitigated against them in order to minimize the business damage they may cause.

Risks can come from a variety of sources: uncertainty in financial markets, labor strikes, execution failures, legal liabilities, credit risk, accidents, natural causes and disasters, loss of key individuals in the business, war, change in the taxation system, and many more. The risk management process must therefore include the following steps to successfully monitor the many potential risks inherent in new product innovation:

Step 1: List all the possible risk factors.

Step 2: Assign a level (low, medium, high) to each factor to indicate how probable it is that it might happen.

Step 3: Assign a level (low, medium, high) to indicate what the impact on the business will be if that risk factor indeed happens.

Step 4: Plan mitigation for at least the highest-priority risk factors: namely, those that scored high in both probability and impact (potential damage). It is also prudent to devote resources to address those factors with medium probability and high impact (damage) as well.

Naturally, new products bring significantly more risk to the table because of the additional unknowns they add. This chapter will focus mainly on risk factors related to new products. In the case of new products, the project manager normally champions risk management. We covered some of the risks in chapter 14, "Synchronize All the Moving Parts." Here, we will dive deeper into additional aspects and different angles.

Market Risk

Market risk may present itself on three fronts in the life of a business and its new product launches: customers' acceptance, competition, and ecosystem readiness. Read through this section to familiarize yourself with these risks, focusing particularly on how to minimize the probability or its occurrence and its potential affects.

Customers' Acceptance

The uncertainty surrounding customer response to your new product or service could come in two ways. On one hand, customers' demand for your venture could be significantly higher than you expected. The risk here is that if you do not fulfill the demand in a timely manner, the customers will go somewhere else. On the other hand, customers' demand could be lower than you expected. The risks to the success of your product launch are painfully obvious in this scenario.

Competition

New product development, by nature, is kept confidential. It is very likely, however, that by the time you launch, you will have more competition than you were aware of when you started out. How can you best prepare for a more crowded marketplace when you launch your new product? Here are three quick actions to take right away.

1. **Budget for industry events, which is a good place to gather intelligence.** The marketing department is the one that usually tracks industry events. The people that are most suitable for this intelligence gathering are people with deep knowledge of the technology at hand who are more likely to read between the lines and extrapolate from partial competitive information they run across.

2. **Sign up to be a member of the relevant industry associations, which is another source of intelligence.** Once again, as above, marketing staff are traditionally the ones who track these activities, but the actual participation is best done by a technical individual. These industry associations normally have regular conference calls, but they also schedule face-to-face meetings. The daylong meeting often ends with a happy hour in a bar, which might be an excellent opportunity for intel gathering. As the saying goes, "When wine sinks, words swim."

3. **Define the product with minimum development risks to minimize schedule slippages.** Designers and engineers are perfectionists. If you are not careful, they will easily sacrifice schedule to add another nice feature to the product. Don't let this happen because being early in the market is often more important than the additional extra features are. We talked about the importance of timely execution in other sections. This is yet another reason why keeping the schedule is so important. This particular task is the project manager's domain. There should be a process for proposing changes to the original product specification, and these proposed changes should be formally reviewed and judged relative to their impact on schedule and product cost.

Ecosystem Readiness

Sometimes, a product's success may depend on other parts of the ecosystem, and if these other parts are not ready to accept it, your launch will be delayed accordingly. If your new product is an innovative construction material, but construction business is down for some reason, most assuredly the ramp up of your product will be impacted (and not for the good).

A firsthand experience from my Motorola days is definitely a good example of this risk.

In the late 1990s, I managed a business unit that provided components for cellular infrastructure equipment. At that time, the common belief was that the cellular world would transition from second-generation (2G) models to third-generation (3G) around 1999, so we started to develop products to support that transition. As often happens in high tech, however, the transition into the new generation didn't happen as quickly as people had expected, and as a consequence, our sales from 3G components were delayed and ramped up only a few years later.

We executed on the new product development. The ecosystem, however, wasn't ready.

People Risk

The people risk in new product or service development may come from one of two directions (or, worst-case, both): One, a bad apple (or apples) on the team. And two, a single point of failure—that is, depending too much on a single member of the team. Let's look at each of these possibilities in greater detail.

1. No matter how brilliant a person is, if he is not a team player, it may ruin the whole project. When hiring people, their technical skills are one thing to test, but equally important—if not more so—are their social skills. The best way to determine someone's emotional intelligence and willingness to contribute to a team is to take these steps. Have a few team members interview the candidate to test for chemistry. Definitely check the references each candidate submits. And have the candidate complete a psychological test where legally allowed as an employment filter. Your HR people will know which tests to apply and where to get them.

2. The risk inherent in a single point of failure means that if the person becomes seriously ill, or quits, it will have an incredibly negative impact on the success of the project. Here are three ways to avert that result.

   a. Hire diverse people with several broad-ranging skills, any one of whom can jump into new shoes—especially a leadership pair—easily.

   b. Create a backup system among the individuals on the team such that each individual has a backup person who can immediately step in to assume his or her responsibilities.

   c. Think big picture. The executive suite and HR should institute a competitive compensation package and career migration opportunities that will minimize the risk of people looking outside the company to improve their situation.

To summarize this discussion of people risk, remember that human capital is one of the most important assets a business has. Making sure that the team operates smoothly and coherently is a delicate job every manager must master.

Technology Risk

In relation to new products, technology risk is the uncertainty inherent in potential technology failure. A technology-related failure could impact the success level of the new product in any or all of three ways.

1. If the product itself is stretching the technology boundaries, and the development hits a roadblock due to an inability to solve a technical challenge inherent in the product itself. This can, and often does, happen mainly in the hi-tech industry. Even when you think your team has solved the technical problem(s) in the lab, the fact that you used state-of-the-art technology could hide many other issues, such as manufacturability problems, quality issues, or unrealistic pricing, to name just a few examples.

What Are the Odds?

Author Andy Weir obviously had technology risk in mind when he wrote his blockbuster novel *The Martian*. In the following passage, two of the twenty engineering experts who had spent twelve hours troubleshooting NASA's multibillion-dollar communications network are explaining to Dr. Venkat Kapoor, director of Mars operations, why they can't figure out a way to talk with marooned astronaut Mark Watney.

"The MAV [Mars Ascent Vehicle] is, like, a communicating *machine*. It can talk to Earth, *Hermes*, even satellites around Mars if it has to. And it has three independent systems to make sure nothing short of a meteor strike can stop communication."

"Problem is," Chuck said, "Commander Lewis and the rest of them took the MAV when they left."

"So four independent communications systems became one. And that one broke," Morris finished.

Venkat pinched the bridge of his nose. "How could we overlook this?"

Chuck shrugged. "Never occurred to us. We never thought someone would be on Mars *without* an MAV."

"I mean, come on!" Morris said. "What are the odds?"

Chuck turned to him. "One in three, based on empirical data. That's pretty bad if you think about it."

Excerpted from the Broadway Books paperback edition (©2014), pages 58–60.

2. Some new products depend on a third-party technological innovation. If that third-party is late in introducing its new product, your product is—to use the vernacular—screwed. A very current example is that if your start-up has developed an app that can work only with a future generation of smart phones, and that future generation is late to market, you have nothing to sell.

3. Don't forget that you depend on technology in your own business processes. Even when you are developing a low-tech product, with no dependency on a technology innovation in its ecosystem, there are always normal technology dependencies in business practices today. Think about a computer failure that could shut down your order system, your appointments calendar, or your phone network, to name but a few migraine-worthy scenarios.

The general rule of thumb for allaying technology risks is to avoid the latest and greatest technology unless you absolutely must use it. In many cases, being one generation behind will be acceptable, and it will keep your launch in a safer place. New products have so many risks attached to them; if there is any risk you can plan to avoid, the safest strategy will indeed be to just circumvent it.

Financial Risk

In the start-up world, financial risk, or money risk, relates to the inability to continue to fund the project. Say, for example, the investors don't put the entire promised amount in the company's bank account. Instead, they divide their commitment into several tranches, each tranche triggered by an execution milestone the investors and the company's management agreed upon. If the company runs out of money before the next tranche is triggered, it is highly likely that it will have to close doors—or continue operations without paying its employees.

A start-up company can minimize such a situation by implementing these steps.

1. Once the execution schedule and budget are agreed upon, manage the operation on a lower budget (obviously without sacrificing your ability to execute steps to achieve the next milestone).

2. In tandem with step 1, focus your energies and activities on execution to attain the next tranche. Sometimes, focusing on the execution from one tranche to another is not the most efficient way long term, but it is the only way to survive the money risk.

3. Find additional funding resources, such as government grants, family and friends, and so on. (Refresh your memory about prospective funding sources by rereading chapter 10, "Funding for a New Product or Service.")

4. Plan some interim revenue source such as part-time consulting work in parallel to the development of the new product.

5. Presell the new product via one of the crowdfunding platforms.

Have a look at this crowdfunding success story for an excellent example of how to implement step 5.

Kingdom Death: Monster 1.5 is a massive cooperative board game. Players must survive a nightmarish, harrowing world by fighting for their lives against an onslaught of terrifying creatures. They will also use objects acquired from battles to build civilizations.

The creator of the game, Adam Poots, raised $2 million on Kickstarter for the original Kingdom Death in 2012. Speaking about the response of crowdfunders to the original game, Poots stated: "The runaway train of success helped pack the game with more original art, in-depth gameplay, and fantastically sculpted minis than even I dreamed of. A game this size could not feasibly be made without the community of supportive backers we found on Kickstarter. It's too expensive to produce and too vivid for distribution. Through the experience of kickstarting Monster, I found a group of people that shares my vision for a blisteringly difficult game with a continually emerging story. I am truly humbled to share it with the world."[1]

His original goal was to raise $100,000. To date, the initiative has secured well in excess of $12 million from more than 19,000 backers, making it the most funded game on Kickstarter and the third most funded business overall.

Financial risk can impact new products in a large corporation just as it can in a start-up. Although the company might have deep pockets, a slowdown in the company's business may cause management to reconsider different ventures the company is involved with, and they may decide to trim down or even kill some of the projects in order to show better results for the next quarter. New products under development have a negative short-term impact on the company's financials, and way too often they are an easy target to kill when the company has to show short-term improvements, even though long term it may hurt the financial performance.

Lost Opportunity Risk

For large corporations, their employees and their customers will come up with new product ideas almost daily. Even the largest corporation cannot execute on all the ideas. Many of them are probably good ones, but resources are limited. Anytime you choose to execute on one great idea, some other possibly equally good ideas, or even better ones, will have to be declined. This is called "lost opportunity risk."

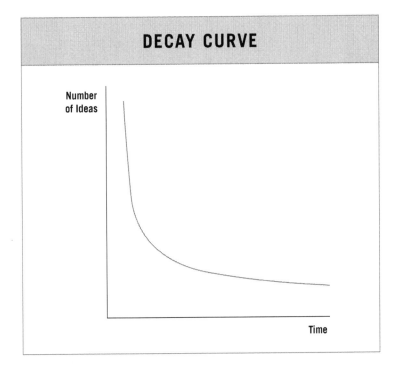

Usually, a company will start with several ideas under consideration. The "decay curve" shown above illustrates the concept of allocating a portion of the budget for initial consideration of multiple ideas, but try to quickly eliminate the ones you don't plan to execute on so that more resources will be freed up to devote to the few projects you do choose to focus on. You might want to implement several exclusion phases. On the marketing side, elimination gates may include a preliminary market study, a detailed market study, sample market tests, and so on. On the implementation side of the formula, feasibility studies may focus on technology risk, production cost, supply chain, and the like. Each of these go or no-go gates should weed out some of the ideas before proceeding to the next round of gates.

Strategies of Managing Risk

At this point, your head is probably reeling from close consideration of the serious risks you undertake in developing any new product or service: market risk, people risk, technology risk, financial risk, and lost opportunity risk. How your business or innovation team will manage those risks may fall into one of the following general categories:

Avoidance: Eliminate the product altogether because the risk is too high, with no acceptable alleviations, or a better risk or reward product wins the elimination process.

Mitigation: Reduce the risk to an acceptable level by reducing the high-risk factors in some way, such as additional market testing, redesigning the product with less risky technology, planning backup to a high-risk supply chain, and so on.

The automotive manufacturing process is very sensitive to supply chain risks. Think about dozens of vehicles moving through the production line, with each vehicle dependent on the readiness of components from hundreds of suppliers. Any supply interruption of one minor component could put the whole line on hold. This means millions of dollars of revenue loss for every day the production line is on hold.

One of the companies I worked with was a major supplier of electronic components to the automotive industry. Our automotive customers made us apply the following risk mitigations to assure smooth continuous supply: Just in time (JIT) warehouse. We had to have our own JIT warehouse next to the customer's factory that was guaranteed to be full all the time, dedicated to supply components to their facility. And second source: We had to guarantee that each component we supplied would be manufactured in at least two different factories. In case one factory went down, the other factory would fill up the demand.

This is business-as-usual supply chain planning. In the case of new products, we had to add these two specific requirements to the development plan for our new component and also to the development plan for the new automobile model that was designed to include our new product.

Risk sharing: Reduce the risk by sharing it with another party, such as a joint venture on product development or a joint venture with a channel partner that will commit to a minimum purchase.

Vital Farms is a food brand with a network of pastured poultry farms. Jason Jones, its principal, described to me that Vital Farms implemented a risk-sharing model with the farmers in their supply chain. The farmers provide the land, buy the hens, and feed them. Vital Farms is committed to buy all the eggs that the farms produce. The farmers' risk is the yield they get from their investment (i.e., the number of eggs produced), while Vital Farms absorbs the market risk of not being able to sell all the eggs they committed to buy from the farmers.

Takeaways

- Any business has uncertainties, as no one can predict the future with 100 percent confidence—or accuracy.

- New products add to the normal business risks because of unknown market acceptance, as well as execution and financial risks related inherently to the new product.

- Before kicking off a new product project, list the different risk factors and plan mitigations for the riskiest ones.

- Don't put all your eggs in one basket.

CHAPTER 18

EXPANSION

There comes a time in the life of each innovation that the potential in the initial target market has been maximized, and if you want to continue to enjoy significant growth, additional expansion strategies must be implemented.

The two most straightforward growth strategies are either to take the same products to new markets or to introduce new products to the same markets. The first strategy benefits greatly from the lessons learned from the initial new product launch, contributing thereafter to repeat launches into new verticals or new territories. The second strategy leverages the relationships you've cultivated with existing customers who value the initial new product. Simply ask them "What else can I do for you?" and implement their wish list.

A third, more difficult, growth strategy is to create new products to take to new markets. Although it is not impossible, it is a significantly riskier route than the other two approaches.

For that reason, I've chosen to explore the two easier growth strategies in the sections that follow.

EXPANSION STRATEGIES

	Same Products	New Products
New Markets	Same Products New Markets	New Products New Markets
Same Markets	Same Products Same Markets	New Products Same Markets

Take the Same Products to New Markets

Employing the strategy of taking the same products to new markets could mean a new market segment or simply a geographic expansion into new territories. (One aspect of market expansion—going global—is so important that I've devoted the entire chapter 22 to it.)

While I managed new products for one of Motorola's business units, we developed a semiconductor chip to go into a remote control key for automobiles. After the initial exclusivity period with the first customer expired, we offered the same chip to populate remote controls for garage door openers and also for TVs.

Sometimes, the new market verticals are discovered by accident. Have a look at this example that no one in the pharmaceutical industry had ever imagined.

Sildenafil is a drug developed by Pfizer Inc. (NYSE: PFE) to treat angina, a heart condition that constricts the vessels that supply the heart with blood. During trials, male volunteers started reporting an unusual side effect: noticeably increased erections.[1]

Pfizer senior scientist Chris Wayman was charged with investigating this side effect. In the lab, he created a model simulating male genitalia. He took a set of test tubes filled with an inert solution, and in each one he placed a piece of penile tissue taken from an impotent man. Each piece of tissue was then connected to a box that, with the flick of a switch, would send a pulse of electricity through the tissue. Applying this electrical current mimics what happens when a man is sexually aroused. The first time Wayman conducted the test, nothing happened to the blood vessels in the tissue. When he added Sildenafil to the tissue bath, however, the artificial penile blood vessels suddenly relaxed, as they would for a man to give him an erection. Following the clinical trial and the discovery that Sildenafil was good for those suffering from erectile dysfunction, Pfizer decided to commercialize the drug, named Viagra, as a remedy for it. The medicine was then patented in 1996.

Two years later, on March 27, 1998, the U.S. Food and Drug Administration approved Viagra's use for treating erectile dysfunction. Later that year, Viagra was available for purchase in the United States. It proved to be a huge success, with recorded sales of the capsules totaling more than $1 billion for the period 1999 to 2001.

Take New Products to the Same Markets

Employing the strategy of taking new products to the same markets could go in either or both of two different directions. One choice is to expand horizontally. For example, if your existing product is running shoes, expanding horizontally could be in the form of other running-related products such as running shorts, running socks, and so on. The other choice is to expand vertically by adding value to existing products. For example, a metal mill that is producing raw material such as metal sheets and metal rods could move up the food chain by making metal pipes, bridge segments, and so on. Note that vertical expansion is a somewhat problematic move, however, because your business may find itself competing with its own customers and upsetting them.

Recall my earlier example about my team at Motorola expanding the list of remote control devices we embedded our new semiconductor chip in. At the same time, we also introduced that new semiconductor to our existing customer base. We enjoyed excellent business relationships with several significant customers in automotive electronics and in consumer electronics whose brands were household names. We leveraged those relationships to develop additional products in partnership with them. These new joint-venture projects offered the twofold benefits of us expanding our portfolio as well as us strengthening the bonds we had established with these customers.

The Case of Tyson Foods

Tyson Foods Inc. (NYSE:TSN) expanded by going in both directions—horizontally and vertically—to grow their business.[2] Here is their success story in a nutshell.

John Tyson bought and raised fifty "springer" chickens on his farm in Springdale, Arkansas, in 1935 and hauled them to Chicago to sell at a profit. Two years later, he named his business Tyson Feed & Hatchery, and the company continued to prosper by buying and selling chickens, aided by the post–World War II boom. For nearly three decades after its inception, Tyson expanded mostly by buying other poultry businesses, still staying focused on selling chicken meats.

In 1969, that began to change. Tyson's first move up the food chain was to acquire Prospect Farms Inc., the company that became its precooked chicken division, which was targeted for institutions and restaurants. By the 1980s, more than half of Tyson's business was with this segment.

In grocery stores, however, Tyson's name was not as popular as that of Holly Farms. After bumpy negotiations and legal disputes, Tyson agreed in 1989 to pay $1.29 billion for Holly Farms, and the company was fully merged into Tyson later that year. In 1990, the first full year with Holly Farms under its wing, Tyson's sales increased by 51 percent. The purchase of Holly Farms made Tyson a very significant player in the chicken industry and put the company in a stronger position in beef and pork.

During the 1990s, Tyson expanded further by acquiring a few seafood suppliers.

In mid-2001, Tyson made its boldest move to diversify. Tyson acquired IBP, the world's largest beef processor, for $4.4 billion, transforming the company from a chicken-only mega operation into the largest diversified meat company in the world. The acquisition made Tyson a $23-billion enterprise, responsible for processing nearly one-quarter of all meat sold in the United States and earned the company a third-place U.S. ranking as a packaged food company, behind Philip Morris's Kraft Foods division and ConAgra (NYSE: CAG).

In 2016, Tyson even invested in an alternative protein supplier named Beyond Meat. Tyson Foods' total revenue that year was $37 billion, with only 30 percent coming from poultry, 37 percent from beef, 11 percent from pork, and 20 percent from prepared food.

In 2017, Tyson Foods was the world's largest processor and marketer of chicken, beef, and pork and is the recognized market leader in almost every retail and food service market it serves. By expanding horizontally into additional non-poultry meats, as well as vertically into prepared food, Tyson managed to more than triple their revenue beyond what the original poultry business contributed.

When you're at an expansion crossroads in which you are deciding between same products to new markets or new products to same markets (or both) you have to make a decision based on your company's strength in each situation. If you are the absolute leader in product X, expanding to other markets will probably be an easier path. If you are the leading player in a defined market, the easier path will be to add products and services to that market. Expanding in both directions is also possible if you have the resources to support both.

Takeaways

- Once the initial target market is maximized, additional expansion strategies must be implemented so your business can continue to enjoy significant growth.

- The two easiest expansion strategies are: Launch the same products to new market segments and/or new territories; and introduce new products for the same markets your business is currently serving.

- Be on the lookout for opportunities to expand horizontally (by offering products related to your innovation) and/or to expand vertically (by adding value to what your business offers and does best).

CHAPTER 19

EMOTIONAL PRODUCTS

Any product satisfies a need. Food products satisfy hunger and the need to maintain a certain level of health and energy. Transportation products satisfy the need to get from point A to point B. An emotional product satisfies an emotional need.

A perfect example is jewelry. Jewelry doesn't have a tangible physical function. It is all about the emotions you feel when you buy it for someone else and when you give or receive it as a gift. When you buy jewelry for yourself, there is an intangible motivation to it (as I describe later in this chapter).

A less expensive example of an emotional product is a souvenir—especially those from exotic places. For example, you buy a Planet Hollywood T-shirt in Paris not because you ran out of clean laundry in the middle of your vacation or business trip. You buy it because you want to impress your friends and family back home that you were in Paris. In most cases, you won't even wear that T-shirt until you return home.

Why Do Customers Buy Emotional Products?

Here are a few explanations of what motivates customers to buy emotional products.[1]

Pride

As we saw in the Planet Hollywood–Paris example, people buy products because they want to be admired, to feel proud of their socio-economic status, and, quite frankly, to show off. If you need to commute to work, you can easily satisfy that need with a $20 thousand vehicle; if you chose to do it with a luxury automobile, your motivation is the need to be admired. A man buys a $5,000 engagement ring to get his girlfriend to say yes. He buys her a $25,000 ring so she can show it off to her coworkers in the office—and polish his image among them all.

Sense of Belonging

We all know the saying "keeping up with the Joneses." You build a swimming pool in your backyard because all your neighbours have one, not because you love hanging out at the pool or you enjoy swimming. You buy your country club's polo shirt because you want to demonstrate your connection to that club, not because you need another shirt. And if membership dues are $1,000 a month, there is also an element of pride in walking around the grounds with that shirt on.

Sex and Romance

Next to the human need for food, sex is one of the strongest motives behind people's response to emotional products. People like to dress in the latest styles and to look smart particularly to attract and please members of the opposite sex (or the same sex in some cases). Consumers purchase perfumes and colognes, lipsticks and eyeliner, toupees and wigs, tattoos and body piercings, sunglasses and tinted contact lenses all in the name of love and being beloved. Going as far back as ancient times, these adornments and beautification rituals are the peacock feathers of humans longing to attract others.

Imitation of Trendsetters

Trendsetters could be sports heroes or entertainment stars or even the cool (aka popular) kids at school. Ordinary folks often imitate the outfits and hairstyles of these celebrities. Imitation of political or business leaders in their dressing style and manners is common too. To appeal to this motive of buyers, savvy marketers often hire popular actors, renowned athletes, and retired politicians to appear in their advertising campaigns.

Being on the Cutting Edge

Some people get great satisfaction from being the first to own a new gadget. They enjoy being the center of attention during the first few weeks or months after a launch, when they are the only ones—or are among the very few—that own the new product, be it as large as a yacht or as small as an earbud. Have you ever asked, "Why would people stand in line for hours to be among the first to own the latest iPhone model when they could buy it in just another couple of weeks when the stores are not so busy?" Here's your answer: Being on the cutting edge is a strong emotional pull that some people just can't say no to.

Love and Affection

Human beings are basically social animals. The emotions of love and affection for their near and dear ones are quite a natural motive behind their buying habits. Often, you buy a gift for a loved one as a way to show your affection for that individual. The "feel good" feeling of love works both ways: You feel good loving others and you feel good being loved. (Recall that this links directly to why people buy jewelry—an emotional product with a dash of pride thrown in for good measure.)

Habits

A habit can be defined as an acquired pattern of behavior that often occurs automatically. Habits are easy to make but difficult to break. In the context of addicting customers to your product (which I discussed in chapter 12, "Launch Time: Marketing," when I mentioned Nir Eyal's book on this subject), this human tendency to develop habits can be used to good advantage by marketers.[2] Once customers are habituated to your products, little or no persuasion is necessary to sell to them repeatedly.

Functional versus Emotional Advertising

Often, the product may be functional, but the motivation underlining a customer's purchase might be emotional. To take our earlier example of buying a piece of jewelry as a gift for your girlfriend, you might buy her a car instead. In this simple example, the car is a functional product, but the buying motivation is emotional. Often, suppliers will play the emotional card when promoting functional products. The list that follows shows different approaches to advertising, comparing emotional ads to functional ads used by makers of competitive products.

What follows are a few comparisons of actual lines used in advertisements, which I've labeled either functional or emotional.

Automobiles

Subaru: Love is in the air (emotional).

Ford F-150: It's simple. Burns less fuel. Burns less cash (functional).

Jaguar used a reverse-logic risky emotional campaign when they unveiled their F series sports car in 2014. The ad featured British actor Tom Hiddleston, looking as dapper and sounding as suave as James Bond but presenting the Jaguar-F as the car of choice for practitioners of the art of villainy.

Watches

Timex: Who cares what time it is. Time is only one dimension of the Timex Ironman watch (functional).

Rolex: Add some elegance to your life (emotional).

Before the advent of digital watches, these timepieces were a once-in-a-lifetime purchase. Today, watches serve different functionalities depending on your lifestyle and hobbies and also as an emotional status symbol accessory, as we saw in the Rolex ad.

Chickens

Tyson: Make dinner more fun with Tyson's chicken nuggets (emotional).

Popeyes: [Get] extra spicy fried chicken from Popeyes (functional).

Jewelry

Tiffany & Co. (NYSE: TIF): In 2015, Tiffany launched a whole campaign based on a couple's relationship—with New York City in the background. They didn't even show any jewelry. They only showed the impact of the jewelry on this couple's relationship.

JCPenney: The department store's "Buy More Save More" campaign encouraged you to spend more on jewelry, with growing discounts as you increased the purchase value of the item you selected.

Several leading jewelry houses rely on their already strong brand and their ads show merely a bold photo of an exceptionally appealing piece of jewelry with their oversized logo next to it. No words are necessary.

Cell Phones—Early and Current Models

One of the best real-life examples of functional products used as emotional status symbol products are the early days of cell phones. The first cell phones were really car phones because they were so big and heavy. The electronics were bulky too because they included a fairly large and heavy base electronics box installed permanently in the car, with a brick-size handset that could not be removed either. It also required that a very visible antenna be installed on your car. I remember buying one for my wife in the early 1990s. It arrived in a heavy two-foot cubic box, and it had to be installed by a special shop trained and licensed by the manufacturer.

The first models of these phones cost thousands of dollars, and placing a local call with them cost about a dollar a minute. In the case of compatible locations in which the phone was serviceable, the roaming cost was several dollars per minute. Clearly, the cell phones of the 1980s and early 1990s were an instrument used only by businesspeople, white-collar professionals, and the wealthy. Having a cell phone in those days was a significant status symbol.

This created a market for mock-up phones and antennas that cost only $10 or $20. People would buy them just to present themselves as cell phone owners, and they hoped to enjoy the perks that came with this status. As to the phones, however, there was no functionality whatsoever.

I was a Motorola executive for twenty years during its glory days, which is to say, I was in the middle of the cell phone revolution. Some of my roles were directly related to cell phones. Motorola was the undisputed commercial cell phone leader from its launch in the mid-1980s until about the mid-1990s. Our number one position was a direct result of our technology leadership in that space.

As the industry started to mature during the 1990s, an unanticipated competition emerged from a totally unexpected angle. Nokia realized that cell phones were becoming a common accessory among young people, and the appearance of the phone played a key role in their decision as to which phone to buy. Choosing a cell phone based on the color of its case is an emotional decision. It has absolutely nothing to do with its functionality as a communication device but everything to do with its function as an appealing fashion accessory.[3]

Nokia's market share skyrocketed from 2 percent in 1995 to more than 40 percent in 2000. (They later lost market share for different reasons, but that is not the purpose of this analysis.) The Nokia/Motorola story is also another excellent example of the orthogonal differentiation, or as W. Chan Kim and Renée Mauborgne call it, "Blue Ocean Strategy"[4] (which I discussed in chapter 6, "Competition: In Business Different Is Often Better than Being Better"). Have another look at the additional coverage of emotional differentiation in that chapter.

Pet Rocks

Now let's take a look at the story of pet rocks, which is a great example of fulfilling emotional needs at multiple levels.[5]

Pet owners completely understand that pets fulfill part of a human being's need to give and receive love. (Some pets serve a functional role too, but that is beyond the scope of this section.) Pets present their owners with an inherent problem, however: they need maintenance, which comes in the form of feeding them, walking a dog a few times a day, changing the litter box for a cat, taking them for checkups at the veterinarian's office, and so forth.

Then, in April 1975, along came marketing executive Gary Dahl in a bar named Bonny Doon. As he sat and listened to his friends complain about their pets, and the work they required, it gave him an idea for the perfect pet: a rock. A rock would not need to be fed, walked, bathed, or groomed, and it would not be disobedient, become sick, or die. Although Dahl joked about it, he nevertheless drafted an instruction manual for a pet rock. The manual was full of gags that referred to the rock as an actual pet.

The Pet Rocks were marketed as if they were live pets, with orders shipped in custom cardboard boxes complete with straw and breathing holes. The fad lasted about six months, ending after a short increase in sales during the Christmas season of December 1975. Dahl sold 1.5 million Pet Rocks for $4 each and became a millionaire overnight.

This idea was later repeated with the introduction of robotic pets in Japan in the late nineties. Sony introduced the first one, named AIBO (for artificial intelligence robot). In 2006, AIBO, described as "the most sophisticated product ever offered in the consumer robot marketplace," was inducted into the Carnegie Mellon University Robot Hall of Fame.

The same concept has further evolved into an AI computerized friend, which either resides in your personal computer or visits you via the Internet.

The need to love and be loved is not new, and neither is the concept of artificial loved ones. Back in the day, and all over the world, they used to be called dolls. Some of the ancient dolls were used as entertainment, as toys, and for spiritual purposes. An ancient Egyptian doll made of wood, for example, dates back to about 2,000 BC.

How B2B Companies Can Use Emotional Marketing Effectively

People don't usually think about B2B decision-making as being emotional; it's supposed to be "all business" after all. Yet it is important to recognize that even in B2B relationships, there is room for emotional play.

In situations where the product may not be an emotional one, the customer's decision may nevertheless be driven by emotions. Emotional marketing moves beyond rational marketing, which focuses just on product functionality attributes to marketing that focuses on capturing a share of the consumer's heart with products that connect on a deep personal and emotional level, with the decision makers at the targeted business.

How can B2B companies leverage such an effective tactic? First, remember that behind every business decision there are humans involved. Therefore, emotion-triggering techniques can still be effective, just with a slightly different twist.

For B2B companies, emotional marketing should appeal to different emotions than the ones consumer purchases do. An Inc.com contributing editor and author of the award-winning blog, Sales Source, Geoffrey James posited seven unique "emotional hooks" that drive B2B buying.[6] Here is my paraphrase of each of those seven categories.

Job Security

The buyer feels "safe" purchasing from you and your firm. IBM salespeople have been using the old saying "You will never be fired for buying IBM" for ages. The same saying can be applied to other strong B2B brands.

Career Advancement

Buyers feel that buying from you and your firm will give them career bonus points or position them better for the next career transition, either inside or outside the current firm. For example, buying a cutting-edge business apparatus because it will look good on their resume the next time they will be in the job market. In the technology industry, customers' employees will gladly experiment with any new gadget presented to them just to make sure they stay current on the latest technology. During my career in hi-tech, any new gadget was always an easy sell because of that reason.

Personal Achievement

Buyers take pride in their work and feel that buying from you and your firm is the right thing to do based on their own self-image as a good person. For instance, buying a product from a supplier that donates a portion of the sale to feed the poor will make you look good in the eyes of your friends and family.

Internal Relationships

The buyer likes the people she's buying from and wants them to be happy. For example, the salesperson is her boyfriend's cousin, and she owes him a favor.

External Relationships

The buyer actually likes the sales rep personally and therefore wants to please him. Or she hates the competitive rep and wants to stiff him by buying elsewhere. No need for an example here.

Easiest Path

The buyer prefers a certain brand just because it is the path of least resistance; therefore, buying it is the least time-consuming path. Vetting a new vendor takes time—time the buyer would much rather spend at home with loved ones.

Simple Greed

The buyer expects to receive some sort of benefit from buying. Warning: This can take the form of a request for an illegal kickback. Other than the illegal kickbacks, there are also hidden semi-legit financial benefits. For example, the users training workshop for the new product will take place at a five-star resort in Hawaii.

When I ran the marketing organization for a Microcontrollers business unit at Motorola, we introduced a new product family that combined standard microcontroller features with added functionality for signal processing. Microcontrollers are tiny computers that are used to control such mechanical systems as a robotic arm or the paper movement in your printer. In some situations, the mechanical control requires signal processing functionality: for example, the controlling of an active shock absorber in your vehicle (that changes its characteristics based on vibrations created by road conditions) or a controller that analyses engine rotations.

Our launch campaign was focused on the theme that the future of mechanical controls was based on signal processing knowledge, and any engineers who chose not to educate themselves on this new technology might find themselves obsolete a few years hence. (This can be categorized as a career-related motivation in reference to the previous list.) The audience was the engineers who were working for our customers, designing mechanical systems with microcontrollers embedded in them. The entire promotion was intended to educate these engineers about this new functionality using a self-learning kit we sold— reinforced by a competition focused on ideas about how to use this new technology in their application. We used this campaign kit for the self-learning exercises the customers were required to go through. The campaign was a huge success. We ended up selling three times the number of kits we expected. Some of these engineers incorporated this new signal processing capability into the new designs that they were responsible for.

This, by the way, is also an excellent example of an unmatched Blue Ocean (or orthogonal) product differentiation because none of our competitors at the time had this signal processing functionality in their microcontrollers.

Some of these examples demonstrate that by adding an emotional angle to it, the perceived value of a functional product can be enhanced.

Estimating the market potential of new emotional products will nevertheless be somewhat challenging.

Takeaways

- In many cases, products fulfill emotional needs.

- Try to find an emotional stimulus even when your company's innovation is not an emotional product.

CHAPTER 20

INTELLECTUAL PROPERTY, TRADEMARKS, AND OTHER RELATED MATTERS

Intellectual property rights (IPRs) are temporary monopoly rights granted to the creators of the intellectual property (IP), and they include patents, trademarks, copyright, industrial design rights, and, in some jurisdictions, trade secrets.

Protect Your Innovations

Each type of IP consists of a number of different rights that sometimes can be difficult to comprehend. The rules for each IPR are also different. What governs patents and inventions, for instance, is different from what governs trademarks (marks that identify goods or services). Copyright is an entirely separate area of the law, as is trade secrets.

In some cultures, the individual who created the IP does not own it; rather, it is considered to be in the public domain. The reasoning is that for many years, both the family and the government have invested in this individual's education, which led to his or her invention; thus, the public has the right to benefit from it, not just the individual. There is some sense in this concept. If we don't provide protection for the innovation, however, businesses will not be motivated to invest in generating new products. If, after your company reveals an innovation, anyone could copy it for a fraction of the original development costs, why would your company continue to make the significant investment to initiate the innovation process?

Here is the motivation underpinning protection of intellectual properties as defined in the U.S. Constitution, Article 1, Section 8: "The Congress shall have power . . . to promote the Progress of Science and useful Arts, by securing for limited Times to Authors and Inventors the exclusive Right to their respective Writings and Discoveries."

As I've stated throughout *Lay an Egg and Make a Chicken Soup*, innovation is the lifeblood of business competitiveness, but without IP protection, your competition can copy your invention very easily and close that competitive gap in no time. The IPRs protect inventors and artists, musicians and moviemakers, and this knowledge should encourage them to create, confident that the monetization of their work is safeguarded.

Merck v. Gilead Hepatitis C Lawsuit

Pharmaceutical R&D is a very expensive process, often approaching a billion dollars. The intellectual property lawsuits in this industry are proportionally high.

Gilead Science Inc. (NASDAQ: GILD) had developed two hepatitis C drugs: Sovaldi and Harvoni. Combined U.S. sales of the two drugs in 2015 were $12.5 billion, with global revenue of $19.1 billion. Harvoni's list price is $1,125 per pill and $94,500 for a twelve-week regimen.

In a 2016 lawsuit Merck & Co. (NYSE:MRK) filed against Gilead (NASDAQ: GILD), the company claimed that Gilead's two hepatitis C drugs infringed on Merck's 2002 patents covering the use of certain compounds to fight hepatitis C infection. In its counterarguments, Gilead tried to claim that Merck's patent wasn't clear about its practical application. The court did not accept Gilead's arguments, and following a nearly two-week trial, the judge found that Merck's patent was valid, and awarded Merck $2.54 billion in royalties.

No matter the ruling, when so much money is involved, the losing party is likely to appeal.

The purpose of this example is not to dive into the complex legal debates (which are beyond our scope here); rather, it's simply to demonstrate the amount of money and effort and length of time that can be spent on defending intellectual property.[1]

The Hangover

In the movie *The Hangover Part II*, Stu Price, a dentist played by actor Ed Helms, wakes up after a night of partying and finds a tribal tattoo wrapped around his left eye. Price's tattoo is identical to the one Mike Tyson has, and it alludes to the boxer's part in the original movie *The Hangover*. Tyson's tattoo artist, S. Victor Whitmill, filed a lawsuit against Warner Bros. Entertainment just weeks before the movie's opening. Since he had obtained a copyright for the eight-year-old "artwork on 3-D," he claimed that the use of his design in the movie without his consent was copyright infringement. Warner Bros., of course, saw it as a parody falling under fair use.

Chief Judge Catherine D. Perry of the United States District Court for the Eastern District of Missouri denied a ban on the movie's release, but she added that Whitmill still had a case. Like most civil lawsuits, Warner Bros. and Whitmill had an out-of-court settlement, the terms of which were not disclosed.

Once again, the purpose of this example is not to turn us into IP experts, but just to demonstrate the amount of money involved. The *Hangover* trilogy revenue has exceeded $500 million (and rising). No wonder, then, that Whitmill expected his contribution to warrant a financial benefit, and Warner Bros. agreed to settle.[2]

A Short IP Lexicon

To repeat the terms and definitions I gave at the beginning of this chapter, intellectual property rights are the rights granted to the creators of intellectual property and include patents, trademarks, copyright, industrial design rights, and, in some jurisdictions, trade secrets. Artistic works, including music and literature, as well as discoveries, inventions, words, phrases, symbols, and designs can be protected as intellectual property.

I recommend that you hire an IP attorney to walk you through the different options and to file the proper papers with the governments of the countries you choose as relevant.

A **patent** is an IPR granted by the government to an inventor, giving the inventor the right to exclude others from making, using, selling, and importing an invention for a limited period of time. An invention is a solution to a specific technical problem, which may be a product or a process, and generally has to fulfill three main requirements: It has to be new, it cannot be obvious, and there needs to be a practical applicability.

A **trademark** is a recognizable sign, design, or expression that distinguishes products or services of a particular trader from the similar products or services of other traders.

A **copyright** gives the creator of an original work the exclusive rights to it, usually for a limited time. Copyright may apply to a wide range of creative, intellectual, or artistic forms, or "works." Copyright does not cover the ideas and information themselves, only the manner in which they are expressed.

An **industrial design right** protects the visual design of objects. An industrial design consists of the creation of a shape, configuration, or composition of pattern or color or the combination of pattern and color, in two-dimensional or three-dimensional form containing aesthetic value, such as is used to produce a product, industrial commodity, or handicraft.

A **trade secret** is a formula, practice, process, design, instrument, pattern, or compilation of information that is not generally known, by which a business can obtain an economic advantage over competitors and customers. There is no formal government protection granted; each business must take measures to guard its own trade secrets.

Confidential information is privileged communication shared with only a few people for furthering a certain purpose. Any receiver of confidential information is prohibited from using it to take advantage of the giver. A nondisclosure agreement (NDA) is a document that offers protection to people engaged in a business relationship where confidential information is shared.

Agriculture **plant breeder's right** is the right to commercially use a new variety of a plant. The variety must, among other things, be new and distinct. In the registration process, the evaluation of the propagating material of the variety is examined.

Just Who Did Invent the Telephone?

Are you aware of the historical dispute (perhaps still ongoing in some circles) about who the true inventor of the telephone is, Alexander Graham Bell or Elisha Gray? It's an interesting story well worth your while.

During the 1870s, Alexander Graham Bell pursued research into a method of telegraphy that could transmit multiple messages over a single wire simultaneously, a so-called harmonic telegraph.

In the summer of 1874, Elisha Gray developed a harmonic telegraph device using vibrating reeds that could transmit musical tones. In December of that year, he demonstrated it to the public at the Highland Park [Illinois] First Presbyterian Church. On February 11, 1876, Gray included a diagram for a telephone in his notebook, and three days later Gray's lawyer filed a patent caveat (an announcement of an invention) with the U.S. Patent Office (USPTO) for the invention. (His original name for this gadget was "An Instrument to Receive and Transmit Vocal Sounds Through Telegraphy.") That same day, Bell's lawyer, Marcellus Bailey, hand delivered a patent application for a harmonic telegraph to the USPTO.

On February 19, the USPTO put Bell's application on hold for three months to give Gray time to submit a full patent application with claims, after which the patent office would begin interference proceedings to determine whether Bell or Gray was the first to invent the claimed subject matter—the telephone.

Nothing was entered in Bell's lab notebook until March 7. Bell's patent was issued on March 7. On March 8, Bell recorded an experiment in his lab notebook, with a diagram similar to that included in Gray's patent caveat application. Bell finally got his telephone model to work on March 10, when Bell and his assistant, Thomas A. Watson, both recorded the famous "Watson, come here" story in their notebooks.

Bell testified under oath that he discussed in general terms Gray's caveat with patent examiner Zenas Fisk Wilber. But this introduces a fishy angle: In an affidavit from April 8, 1886, Wilber admitted that he was an alcoholic who owed money to his longtime friend and Civil War Army companion Marcellus Bailey (Bell's lawyer, remember). Wilber says that after he issued the suspension on Bell's patent application, Bailey came to visit him. In violation of USPTO rules, Wilber told Bailey about Gray's caveat and told his superiors that Bell's patent application had arrived first.

(Note: You'll have noticed that these dates don't always

make sense. And there are those who argue that Bell's diagrams are after-the-fact fabrications. I am not trying to take sides here; I just want to demonstrate the importance of timely patent filing, allocation of money to do it, having the right connections, and having the right legal team to support you.)

To add to the confusion, Antonio Meucci, an Italian immigrant, began developing the design of a talking telegraph or telephone in 1849. In 1871, he filed a caveat for his design of a talking telegraph, long before Gray and Bell. Due to financial hardships, however, Meucci could not renew his caveat. His role in the invention of the telephone was overlooked until the United States House of Representatives passed a Resolution on June 11, 2002, honoring Meucci's contributions and work in the invention of the telephone.

Timing, money, connections. Has your business secured all three—along with exercising your IPRs—for your new innovative products or services?

Takeaways

- Intellectual property rights (IPRs) are temporary monopoly rights granted to the creators of IP, and they include patents, trademarks, copyright, industrial design rights, and, in some jurisdictions, trade secrets.

- The motivation behind IPRs is to encourage businesses to invest in innovation by protecting their new products or services from being copied by their competitors.

CHAPTER 21

BOARD OF DIRECTORS AND CORPORATE INNOVATION

A board of directors oversees the activities of an organization. Let's start with a brief review of the traditional board roles before we discuss the innovation angle. You may skip the first part if you are familiar with how boards of directors customarily work.

Customary Governance Duties of Corporate Boards

Different types of entities (public company, private company, start-up, nonprofit, and family business, among others) and different industries may have slightly different board structures. We will start with a brief description of the board of directors' roles in general and then drill down into their involvement with the innovation process.

- Governing the organization by establishing broad policies and setting out strategic objectives
- Selecting, appointing, supporting, and reviewing the performance of the chief executive (The titles of this position vary from organization to organization: they are most often chief executive officer, president, or executive director.)
- Terminating the chief executive
- Ensuring the availability of adequate financial resources
- Approving annual budgets
- Monitoring the organization's performance and reporting it to the stakeholders
- Setting the compensation and benefits of senior management

The legal responsibilities of boards and board members vary with the nature of the organization and between jurisdictions. For companies with publicly traded stock, these responsibilities are typically much more rigorous and complex than for those of other types.

Typically, the board chooses one of its members to be the chairperson, who holds whatever title is specified in the bylaws or articles of association.

In some European and Asian countries, there are two separate boards: an executive board for day-to-day business and a supervisory board for supervising the executive board. In these countries, the CEO (chief executive or managing director) presides over the executive board, and the chairman heads the supervisory board, and these two roles will usually be held by different individuals.

Larry Stybel is cofounder and president of Stybel Peabody & Associates (a Lincolnshire International Company). Stybel specializes in corporate governance and leadership change. His other company, Board Options Inc. (BoardOptions.com), is a wealth of information about boards of directors. Larry uses a clever, short guideline for board members about their role: "Nose in—fingers out." He's referring to the distinction between a board's obligation to stick its nose in a company's governance matters but to keep its fingers out of the management of the company.

A board of directors of a large corporation often has several standing committees, such as Audit Committee, Compensation Committee, Nomination and Corporate Governance Committee, Corporate Responsibility Committee, Risk Policy Committee, and more. These committees may vary from one company to another. Some companies may have special-purpose committees based on the specific issues they choose to address.

The board of directors represents the shareholders of the company and oversees the CEO's performance. Some companies may choose to have an advisory board, which does not govern and does not represent the shareholders. Instead, the role of the advisory board is to be a resource for the CEO in issues he or she seeks help on, such as technology feedback, introductions to investors, introductions to customers, government relations, legal advice, and more (as needed).

Governance Duties with Implicit Innovation Aspects

The involvement of the board of directors in the new products or services process varies depending on the nature of the company and the significance of the new products to the overall business strategy. A VC-backed start-up is all about the new product the company was founded to develop and commercialize. In this case, the board of directors is very involved in the new product's strategy and its execution. A start-up board of directors normally consists of representation by its investors and representation of its founding team.

Most boards of directors of larger companies, however, shy away from being involved with the innovation process because they view it as a day-to-day operational topic. Nevertheless, even if they don't devote targeted attention to innovation, several governance duties of the board encompass implied innovation aspects, such as strategy, risk, auditing, management performance, compensation, and CEO transition.[1] As these are critical to every business at every stage of its growth, let's look at each innovation aspect in greater detail.

Strategy

Boards generally highly rate their role as company strategy reviewers. These strategic issues are often discussed when board approval is required for major investment decisions. A soda company doesn't seek its board of directors' approval for every new flavor it creates, but it will most likely require the board's approval if the company's management recommends adding solid food items to its portfolio. The board is entitled to expect management to communicate its actual priorities and provide an estimate of the resources the company is planning to invest by type of innovation.

Risk

Boards have a fiduciary responsibility vis-à-vis shareholders to be the guardians of the company's risks. In some cases, the risks are financial in nature, and the board's audit mission aims to address them. In certain industries and companies, other risks—among them environmental risk and political risk—are regularly reviewed and assessed by the board. In some industries—especially the pharmaceutical industry—the product liability and class action risks are important subjects of board review. Other companies identify innovation risks, which usually fall into three categories. The first category is the risk of not innovating enough and being bypassed by a competitor's new product or service. The second category is the risk of timely innovation execution, such as in meeting the R&D schedule and budget. The third category is the risk of market acceptance of the new product. Board members themselves do not always have to see the emerging trends, but their governance function requires that they ask management to keep a lookout and report to them.

Auditing

Besides their traditional focus on financial audits, boards are gradually extending the range of their supervisory auditing missions beyond the financials. As I've preached in this book many times, *innovation is a critical ingredient to business survival in the long run*; thus, innovation should be included in the list of the board's auditing missions. It is indeed within the legitimate role of the board to ask top management to set a few critical innovation effectiveness measures, which its members can regularly review and discuss thereafter with management. In technology-intensive companies, the level of R&D expenditures—in absolute terms and as a percentage of sales—is a classic example of one such innovation input indicators, but there are others to be considered. Similarly, a frequently measured innovation output indicator is the percentage of sales achieved through new products. Companies such as Medtronic, Hewlett Packard, and Logitech measure and communicate about this ratio regularly at each board meeting.

Management Performance

A critical role of the board is to evaluate the performance of the CEO and the top management team as a basis for decisions on compensation packages and for the replacement of the CEO. To do this, some companies use elaborate sophisticated formulas that resemble the traditional balanced-scorecard concepts used by many human resources departments. CEO scorecards usually combine financial figures and targets—generally based on company growth, profitability, and stock price, among other metrics—with other qualitative or quantitative measures or specific goals pertaining to the company's strategic initiatives and priorities: for example, specific turnaround targets, progress in globalization efforts, capital efficiency improvements, and so on. Companies that depend on the introduction of critical— that is, "make or break" new products (think of Boeing with its 787 Dreamliner, mentioned in chapter 8, "Technology and R&D")—generally include the review of these large projects in the board's deliberation. In these companies, the board will most likely make the compensation packages of the CEO and the top management team contingent on the successful completion of critical new product innovation milestones.

Compensation

The Compensation Committee on most boards of directors is responsible for overseeing the company's compensation programs. These include, among other subjects, developing and monitoring a strategy or philosophy regarding executives' compensation; ensuring regulatory, accounting, and listing compliance; reviewing and approving compensation adjustments for the CEO and executive officers; and assuring the competitiveness of executive compensation.

When structuring the executives' incentive plan, a possible metric to use could be the R&D or sales ratio; another possible one is revenue from new products as a percentage of sales.

If part of CEO compensation is based on stock performance, provide an incentive based on the average stock price for five years or based on year-over-year stock price increase. This will be an important signal to the CEO regarding the value of long-term stock performance (which could greatly be fueled by the company's innovation performance) versus short-term stock performance, in which case the CEO will be incentivized to improve short-term results while sacrificing long-term goals.

CEO Transition

The selection and recruitment of a new CEO is undoubtedly one of the board's most visible and difficult responsibilities. A subject that has captured a lot of attention from the business media is the decline in a CEO's tenure at many an industry giant in recent years. People—CEOs included—spend less time on the job than they did fifty, or even twenty, years ago. I allude to this not to point out any recent wrongdoing, but only as an observation about a general social change.

Boards generally feel more comfortable with the more predictable CEOs than with the innovative, but sometimes more erratic, ones. But new CEOs often need to challenge the status quo and set the company on a new course to maximize a new growth opportunities.

Just listen to the opening salvo of Cisco's (NASDAQ: CSCO) press release when they announced Chuck Robins as their new CEO in July 2015: "Today's pace of change is exponential. Every company, city, and country is becoming digital, navigating disruptive markets, and Cisco's role in the digital transformation has never been more important. Our next CEO needs to thrive in a highly dynamic environment, to be capable of accelerating what is working very well for Cisco, and disrupting what needs to change . . ."

The press release further acknowledged that "Cisco is in a very strong position." Yet despite their strong position, the board of directors realized that their CEO would need to be exceedingly good in leading change.

The Advent of Innovation Committees

Companies must reinvent themselves (or die). IBM (NYSE: IBM), Nucor (NYSE:NUE), and Wipro (NYSE:WIT) bear only the faintest resemblance to their founding forms—and boards ought to be at the forefront of such transformations. New products are the province of R&D teams, but new strategies and structures are squarely in the board's domain.

Some boards have taken the principle further by forming their own innovation committees. The directors of Procter & Gamble (NYSE:PG), for instance, have established an Innovation and Technology Committee; the board of chemical maker Clariant (SWISS: CLN) has done the same; and Pfizer (NYSE:PFI) has created a Science and Technology Committee.[2]

Diebold (FRANKFURT: DBD), a $3-billion company that makes ATMs and a host of related products, was founded in 1876, way before ATMs were invented. The company has survived far longer than most major manufacturers because of a readiness to embrace new technologies, and its directors hope to ensure that the company incorporates new technologies to survive another hundred years.

In 2013, Diebold recruited a new CEO, Andy W. Mattes, who had previously led major business units at Hewlett-Packard, Siemens, and other technology companies. And then, in conducting its annual self-evaluation, the board decided to form a board committee to work with the new CEO on technology and innovation. With the concurrence of the new CEO, the directors created a Technology Strategy and Innovation Committee with a full-blown charter requiring its directors to "provide management with a sounding-board," to serve as a "source of external perspective," to evaluate "management proposals for strategic technology investments," and to work with management on its "overall technology and innovation strategy." When Diebold executives began looking for new technologies it might buy, the Technology Strategy and Innovation Committee—rooted in tech start-up and VC communities—helped the CEO and his staff connect with those who would know or own the emergent technologies that could allow Diebold to strengthen its current lines and buy into the right adjacent lines. As a result, Diebold made such significant acquisitions as Germany-based Nixdorf and Canadian-based Phoenix Interactive Design.

Facebook (NASDAQ: FB), a major multibillion-dollar public social media technology company, is still rooted in its early days as a technology start-up, defining in 2017 the official role of its chairman and CEO, Mark Zuckerberg, to be "responsible for setting the overall direction and product strategy for the company. He leads the design of Facebook's service and development of its core technology and infrastructure."

The impact of innovation on shareholders' equity can be best demonstrated by this example. Intel announced on September 18, 2017, their progress on a new generation of technology called 10nm, information about its technical details, and their commitment to shipping the first commercially available product in this technology. Intel stock immediately responded with a 34 percent increase in less than two months, which added $60 billion to its shareholders equity.

Takeaways

- Innovation is a major ingredient in a company's competitive and survival strategy. Therefore, it must be one of the board of directors' governance responsibilities.

- Board members and committees must remember to restrict their involvement to a "Nose in–fingers out" process.

CHAPTER 22

GOING GLOBAL

R ecall that in chapter 18, "Expansion," I described two of the easiest growth strategies for businesses. One involves taking the same products to new markets, and the other involves taking new products to the same markets. Going global is a special case of the first strategy (same products to new markets), and I think it's important enough to have its own chapter.

Going global has multiple benefits. First, it grows revenue and profits by increasing the total available market (TAM). Additional benefits could be a more efficient supply chain in cases where critical suppliers are outside of your home territory. The other is diversification and risk reduction because your business will be less dependent on a single country. Last but not least, you'll be able to attack your competitors on their home turf in cases where your competitors are from other countries.

Today, globalization is a common "business as usual" practice, but it's not always done at the same time in all regions. Companies may choose to launch only in one territory to better contain the launch, and later on, they expand to other markets as they gain experience and confidence.

The many lessons to be learned from taking your same products to new markets are showcased vividly in the story of what happened when two of America's fast-food giants took their burgers abroad. I'm talking about comparing Burger King's global strategy to that of McDonald's entry into Italy.[1]

McDonald's Expansion into Italy

McDonald's (NYSE:MCD) really worked hard to adapt their restaurant model to the Italian culture without losing the essence of their business strategy.

Having ventured onto Italian soil in the mid-1980s, McDonald's, with its golden arches, can now be seen in nearly every train station, bus station, and airport in Italy. Whereas Americans are always on the move and mostly in their vehicles, in which case a drive-thru model fits best, Italians are on the move as pedestrians in the street or as passengers on public transportation. The easy-in, easy-out strategy employed by McDonald's in the United States is seen in Italy too, but it's been adopted to accommodate that Italian lifestyle. Customers can grab a quick meal to go on their way to or from their train with no hassle and at little cost.

There's a strange dichotomy between the all-Italian language menu, the prices in Euros, and the special Italian menu options all offered in a setting featuring the same McDonald's uniforms, logos, and brand images we are familiar with in the States. In the same vein, McDonald's made some additions to their regular menu to appeal more to Italian interest. To much fanfare, they introduced two different "McItaly" burgers to capture the market for hamburgers, their biggest seller back home, by making them more Italian and less American, boasting such Italian ingredients as olive oil, pancetta, and Asiago cheese to cater to Italian tastes. They've been a big success in Italian locations.

McDonald's did not succeed in Italy by simply transplanting a restaurant from the USA into the heart of Venice. But they were able to change just enough to be accepted and liked by the Italian public over time while maintaining their core business competencies. In Italy, you find armchairs, wooden coffee tables, and dimmer lighting. The seating areas are arranged in small groups instead of row after row of metal tables under bright white surgical lights. There are quiet nooks and crannies in which to relax, chat, work on a computer (thanks to the free Wi-Fi), and read the newspaper—giving these restaurants more of a coffeehouse feel.

Mickey D's took their "same products to a new market" with just enough adjustments to fit seamlessly with that new environment.

Going Global with Help from Your Friends

Unless your company has significant experience doing business in a new country, it is mandatory that you hire an expert to conduct the preparation studies. It is also absolutely necessary to have people on the ground working for you in the other country— people who know the local ecosystem and can navigate your interests through it, as well as react on the spot to any situational changes.

Checklist for Global Expansion[2]

1. **Should the company establish business in foreign markets?** The answer is yes in the following cases:

   a. The company saturated the local market.

   b. The local market is too small to start with.

   c. Other foreign countries are better suited to be buyers of the company's products or services.

2. **Business model:** What business model will the company use in its international development? Should we start with a rep? A distributor? Or establish a subsidiary? Or a joint venture with a local entity?

3. **Which countries:** Which foreign countries present the best opportunity for the company? Some considerations to take into account are need of products, local competition, potential market size, distance, language and culture, time zone, and so on.

4. **Product and business process localization:** Each country has its own legal, cultural, technical, and business requirements. How will the company's product and business process need to be changed (localized) in each foreign country to comply with these?

5. **Core company standards:** Regardless of changes made in the localization process in each country, the company should maintain core elements of its culture in every country in which it operates. What are the core elements of the company's business and culture that it wants to maintain in every country?

6. **Tax and entity planning:** Structure the company's business entities to protect the parent from legal liability, achieve tax efficiency, and streamline treasury function.

7. **Protection of intellectual property:** IP laws are different in different countries. Make sure that you secure your IP protection from the destination country. Also make sure that the other country's IP system will not make it easier for a local competitor to steal your IP.

8. **Tariff and trade laws:** Check if or what import taxes will apply to you. These could be hefty in some cases and make your product too expensive in the destination country. One common way to handle this is to enter into a joint venture with a local entity that contributes enough local content to eliminate or significantly reduce the important tax. The other thing to watch for in your home country is any change to regulations in regard to exports to some other countries.

9. **Legal compliance:** Hire an international attorney or a local attorney from your target market to review your product or service vis-à-vis the local rules and regulations. These can be anything related to public health, safety, medical system regulations, labor laws, animals rights, and so on.

10. **Cultural correctness in the new country:** Your product may be totally legit and acceptable in your home country, but it may be considered offensive or inappropriate in other cultures. For example, Hooters may be totally unacceptable in some cultures because of the revealing dress code of its serving staff. McDonald's in Israel modified the menu in many of their locations there to comply with kosher dietary laws, while their locations in Pakistan are in compliant with Muslim's Halal dietary laws.

No place was more critical than during events surrounding the 2014 international dispute over Ukraine, which prompted a number of Western governments to apply sanctions against individuals, businesses, and officials from both Russia and Ukraine. Sanctions were approved by the United States, the European Union (EU), and a few other countries and international organizations. A few months after, the Russian government responded with counter-sanctions against these countries, including a total ban on food imports from the European Union, United States, Norway, Canada, and Australia. This included fruit, vegetables, meat, fish, milk, and other dairy imports. The sanctions caused economic damage to a number of European Union countries, with the total losses estimated at €100 billion (as of 2015).

Grafski Consulting helps international firms enter the Russian marketplace and develop business in and with Russia. In my communications with the company's founder, Stanislav Grafski, I learned that one of Grafski's clients was an EU cheese maker whose exports were immediately halted upon Russia announcing its government's counter-sanctions. Stan Grafski identified peers in this industry on the ground in Russia and selected the one that had a long-established market share in cheese production and distribution. This Russian cheese manufacturer accepted Grafski's client's offer for a joint venture, with new product manufacturing (i.e., new production lines with new products were launched, thus dramatically increasing the range of products for sale). The latter allowed this new venture to immediately set up local operations in Russia using existing distribution channels, which was up and running only four months later.

This is a good example of how change in the political environment can impact business, but, more importantly, it also shows how having a knowledgeable adviser on the ground in the target country can help significantly with quickly adapting to changing conditions. The success enjoyed by Grafski's client couldn't have been accomplished without his having boots on the ground in Russia.

Takeaways

- The main reason to go global is to expand your business's market potential.

- Going global creates logistical and cultural challenges that are best overcome by having boots on the ground in the target territory.

CHICKEN EVOLUTION

Confucius wisely stated, "Study the past if you would define the future." That's why I've included striking examples from ancient to modern history throughout the chapters in *Lay an Egg and Make Chicken Soup*. Those stories of the rollout of real-world products and services provide an excellent foundation for this look ahead.

Innovation is all about predicting future business opportunities and, even more so, creating them. In this conclusion, I'm not attempting to predict the future so much as looking at different trends in an attempt to extrapolate beyond the short-term horizon. No hard statements, these are only my observations about what the current trends are pointing us toward.

Time and Speed

Speed, or frequency of events, has increased dramatically in recent years. Recall from Physics 101: Time and speed are interrelated. The faster you do something, the less time it takes. One obvious vector is time reduction. Time that it takes to communicate. Time that it takes to move from point A to point B.

Technology helps overcome distance and the time it takes to cover the distance. Humans have evolved from walking, to riding horses, to driving automobiles, to traveling on trains, to flying on airplanes within the past hundred years or so. With technology you don't have to go from point A to point B in order to visit with a loved one or business contact.

There are physical limitations to just how fast you can move, however. That led to inventions of the telegraph, followed by the phone, followed by the videophone—all of which reduce the need to be physically present in order to communicate with another person. Extrapolating this trend, virtual reality will become so real that it could completely replace the need for physical travel. Time will be reduced to the speed of the VR signal to move from point A to point B, which is practically almost zero. The experience will be completely real.

Once this is accomplished, the next time reduction will be creating a VR experience that allows you to be in multiple places simultaneously. How about that?

Possible Business Impacts of Time and Speed Innovations

- How will they affect transportation?
- Virtual tourism?
- Globalization?

- Human relationships? (Will we have remote virtual mar-
  riages? VR family reunions?)

- Entertainment? (Will we attend events virtually? Will
  we take superfast flights to a remote concert and back the
  same evening?)

- Virtual professional services of any kind? Virtual class-
  rooms? Virtual medical care?

- Instant pizza delivery? (Waiting thirty minutes still isn't
  fast enough for me.)

Information

The "information explosion" is the rapid increase in the amount
of available information or data and how this abundance leads to
problems in managing it. "Information overload" is the inability
to digest the growing amount of data at your fingertips. This
requires tools that help you make sense of all it all.

This increase in information triggers several other trends.

Specialization: The increased amount of information can be
somewhat managed through specialization. We've witnessed
this trend over many years in all professions, be it medicine,
engineering, or teaching, to name a few. The more specialized
a professional is, the smaller proportional slice of that overall
information she needs access to. When you are too specialized, there might not be enough business in your home community. Improved VR technology, however, will help expand
your business horizons virtually.

Technology: As the sheer volume of information grows, technology comes to the rescue. Think back to the invention of writing thousands of years ago, through the invention of print, all the way to the Internet and search engines. Today's buzzword for this software category is "big data." Big data refers to a class of tools that are able to analyze extremely large data sets to find relationships and trends between all the data points.

Keep in mind that the "big" in big data is a moving target. What is considered big today will be child's play in the near future. Ultimately, think about a big data machine that will investigate every atom in the universe and predict what will happen to you five years from now at 9:17 in the morning.

Possible Business Impacts of Information

- Ultra-specialized service providers. (This will have to be virtual because oftentimes there are not enough specialty customers locally.)
- Crowd-based medicine. (Big data will be used for diagnostics.)
- Crowd-based poultry health tracking. (This includes using different sensors in the pen and on each bird's body, as well as sensors to analyze its digestive system.)
- Big data–based business forecasting. (Businesses will no longer make decisions based on a small sample, but rather a big data machine will be able to analyze the entire population.)
- Big data–based insurance policies. (Calculating risk and premiums will be based on entire populations.)

Health and Medicine

Life expectancy of prehistoric humans was twenty to thirty years. In the 1700s it was thirty to forty years, and now, in the twenty-first century, it exceeds eighty years for men and women. The statistics are skewed by infant mortality rates over the course of human evolution. Another parameter that shifts the averages is premature death from accidents and injuries that became infected or from contaminated food or water. The survival rates from such injuries or contaminations have increased because of modern medicine, thus adding years to the average lifespan. Last but not least, advances in medical research have translated into new cures for more illnesses, adding years at the tail end of people's lives.

Two major medical advances are cloning and organ regeneration through stem cells. Here is a wild idea that theoretically is pretty realistic today: Clone every person on Earth, keep the cloned embryos in some kind of storage, and revive them when the time comes to pass the longevity baton to the cloned person. Is it considered the same person? Or is it a different person now? Well, we don't have to go that far. It is enough to create a library of cloned body parts and replace any ill body part with its cloned spare. If cost and politics weren't an issue, this could be done today.

Possible Business Impacts of Health and Medicine

- Body parts cloning.
- Elder services.
- Resource utilization because of population explosions.

- Premium health insurance that will cover out-of-the-norm expensive treatments.
- Alternative socioeconomic taxation structure to fund the longer life.

Socialization

Humans are social beings. Many businesses and inventions throughout history have had to do with putting people together physically. Anything from religious congregations to match-makers, from sports games to sports bars fulfill this desire. On the technology front, all the communications from telegraphs to videophone calls to social media are also contributing to putting people in touch with each other—albeit virtually.

This is an emotional business. One of the challenges on this front is to quantify the value before starting such a business. The supply-demand elasticity will define how much of a socializing service people will buy. When an international phone call was $7 per minute, I used to call my family oversees once a week. Years later, when it was a few cents per minute I called oversees an unlimited number of times, for as long a chitchat as we wanted to have. Social media is free to join, so very quickly everybody joined. The monetization for social media providers comes from advertising and premium services.

Possible Business Impacts of Socialization

- Combine social media with virtual reality to make the experience more real.

- Make social events virtual realities. A VR class reunion? A VR cocktail party? VR golfing?
- Big data matchmaking?
- Have VR church services?
- VR club memberships?

Globalization

Four thousand years ago, globalization started with international trade between different nations in the Middle East. Silk Road trade between China, India, Africa, and Europe is recorded as far back as 200 BC. The process continues today, with most large corporations having significant operations in many countries.

For instance, General Electric's business outside of the United States grew from 31 percent of the company's revenue in 2001 to 59 percent in 2011. The proportional ratio of domestic U.S. business shrunk accordingly, and as a result, the absolute volume of General Electric in the States shrunk from $43 billion in 2001 to $28 billion in 2011.

Looking at world changes in the past fifty years, we can identify three major trends.

1. Many small ethnic groups are fighting for their own independent state and will get it sooner or later. Thus, the number of countries is still growing. This process will continue.

2. Borders are getting increasingly porous, and movement of trade, people, and information is so much easier today than it was thirty to fifty years ago. This trend will

continue in the long run. Though politicians will attempt to limit it, their policies will probably be but temporary situations in the grand scale of our long-term future.

3. Regional alliances such as the EU, NAFTA, and Pacific Alliance, to name but a few, will continue to be formed.

The relative dominance of post–World War II major powers is diminishing. This is not to say that their absolute power is being reduced, but the gap with other countries is being reduced thanks to advances in these developing countries. Extrapolating this trend, it is reasonable to predict that the power differential between major nations will flatten.

Possible Business Impacts of Globalization

- Business without borders.
- Businesses will have employees who are cross-culturally fluent. Communications will offer cross-cultural translations.
- Travel and tourism will increase (but some of it may be virtual).
- The field between today's emerging economies and the developed ones will be leveled.

Urbanization

Urban populations worldwide grew from 30 percent in 1950 to 40 percent at the turn of the twenty-first century. According to

United Nations studies, they are expected to exceed 60 percent by 2050. This urbanization happened by expanding the boundaries of the cities horizontally as well as expanding vertically by adding taller and taller high-rises.

The vertical growth of buildings creates a mixed-use development (called a "vertical town"), which blends residential, commercial, cultural, institutional, or entertainment uses. Those functions are physically and functionally integrated, and that provides pedestrian connections. Mixed-use developments can take the form of a single building, a city block, or an entire neighborhood.

Possible Business Impacts of Urbanization

- Reduction in commuters as more people will be working in the same building or block where they live.
- Smart buildings and smart cities.
- Air quality improvement opportunities, indoor as well as outdoor.
- Population safety (fire hazards, earthquakes, rescue, etc.).
- Elevator technology and optimizations.
- Urban farming.
- Basic services in each vertical town (police, medical clinic, post office, school, convenient store, etc.).

328 Lay an Egg and Make Chicken Soup

Artificial Intelligence

Artificial Intelligence (AI) has been a buzzword for many years. Traditional computer programming uses very predictable step-by-step algorithms. The ultimate goal of the AI field is to emulate human thinking, such as intuition, natural language processing, creativity, unexpected problem solving—not to mention such human emotions as joy, sadness, and frustration, to name a few examples.

Despite the many advances that have been made in the AI field over the years (think of limited speech recognition, machines that play chess, or driverless cars), it is still ions away from being able to mimic a human brain. The human brain is a massively parallel, associative, analog machine. Computers are digital and must be preprogrammed for the target tasks. AI scientists are trying to overcome this fundamental difference by taking advantage of improvements in computer processing speeds as well as running multiple computers in parallel. Nevertheless, they are nowhere near the massively parallel processing that occurs even in a small and limited chicken brain.

Scientists are starting to create limited capacity AI capabilities.[1] Where will that take us ten years from now? One hundred years from now? A thousand years into the future? What level of intelligence will the "I" bring to the table? Will it be able to replicate Einstein's brain (and continue his scientific creativity)? Will it be able to mimic Beethoven? Picasso? Churchill? Lenin? Nelson Mandela? If so, on the other, scary side of that coin, will it recreate historical monsters like Hitler or Stalin?

A close adjacent technology to AI is robotics. When the AI results in a mechanical movement of any kind, it connects to a robot to perform that mechanical movement the AI brain wants it to perform. Robots are pretty pervasive today in many applications, such as hazard environment, medicine, manufacturing, and many more. It is likely to evolve even more.

This will be a gradual evolution. Short-term, it is easy to predict the emergence of more intelligent home appliances, artificial pets, self-driving vehicles, and artificially intelligent kitchen robots.

Here are few long-term options to think about:

- Will countries be run by a computerized cabinet of AI beings?

- Will we have an AI judge in court?

- Will it be able to duplicate a spirit of a loved one and have it available for his or her friends and family to continue to enjoy his or her AI replica?

- Will AI discover God and stop religious wars?

- Will it be able to replicate my brain and write my next book for me?

- Will AI take over humanity?

- Do we need to plan ahead and create safety measures to prevent AI from taking over humankind?

The poultry industry is one that showcases the evolving use of AI and robotics. Among the multitudinous chores that robots can assist with are these: Poultry houses require nearly constant attention—cleaning, sanitizing, collecting eggs, and checking on the hens and roosters. This is time-consuming, monotonous work, but it would not bother a robot. Additionally, robots are more precise, thorough, and honest about the work they do compared to their human counterparts.[2]

Will we be able to develop the technology to lay eggs by machines without the need of a chicken?

ACKNOWLEDGMENTS

As I mentioned in the introduction, the material for this book is a combination of textbooks on the different topics, public case studies, and my own experience (which is largely the collective knowledge of all the people I have worked with over the years). In addition, I interviewed several executives on specific topics. I would like to thank the following people for the time and insights they contributed to make this book a success:

Najib Abusalbi, PhD, Director, Corporate University Relations, Schlumberger Limited

Mike Cockrell, CFO, Sanderson Farms

Josh Danziger, Cofounder, SystemX Media

Louise Epstein, Managing Director, Innovation Center at Cockrell School of Engineering, University of Texas–Austin

Stanislav Grafski, Founder, CEO, and Managing Partner, Grafski Consulting

Erik Huddleston, CEO, TrendKite

Ori Kirshner, Head of Samsung VC Israel

Larry Stybel, Cofounder, Stybel Peabody Associates Inc. and Board Options Inc.

Jason Jones, Principal, Vital Farms

A special thanks to Clint Greenleaf, who contributed at two levels: A former publisher, Clint coached me through the book publishing process, and he also agreed to be interviewed as the cofounder and CEO of HomePlate Peanut Butter.

Among the many others I'd like to acknowledge are:

My immediate family: Etty Brish, owner of ELB-Design, who provided tips throughout the process and featured in a couple of examples; Eldor Brish, MD, who was interviewed for the pharmaceutical business model; and Liron Brish, CEO of FarmDog, who did a tremendous job tackling the tedious review of the almost final manuscript, catching many of my sentences that needed improvement and correction.

My great editor, Linda W. O'Doughda, who had the tough job of understanding the vision of partially baked material and provided her valuable guidance to make this book a tasty chicken soup.

My wonderful designer, Sheila Parr, for dressing up this work, for a good dish must also be pleasant to the eye.

Lindsey Clark put some final touches that without them it would have looked too amateur piece.

Last but not least, my early beta readers, who took the risk of being the early taste testers of the chicken soup I made.

CHECKLIST FOR NEW PRODUCT EVALUATION		
Item	**Answer**	**Action**
Describe the idea.		
1 **What need does it solve?**		
How do people address the same need today?		
2 **Do the basic technologies needed available to us today?**	Yes	
	No	Add technology development or technology acquisition to your business plan.
3 **What is the total available market?**		
What is the total serviceable market? Explain.		
Best-case market share?		
Most likely market share?		
Worst-case market share?		
4 **List the ecosystem must haves.**		
Ecosystem item #1 ready?	Yes	
	No	What do we need to make it happen?
Ecosystem item #2 ready?	Yes	
	No	What do we need to make it happen?
Ecosystem item #3 ready?	Yes	
	No	What do we need to make it happen?
***Add more items to the list if needed.		
5 **What price will the market pay for it?**		
What will the cost be?		
Does the market price vs. cost make it profitable?	No	What can be done to reduce cost? What can be done to increase value?
	Yes	

CHECKLIST FOR NEW PRODUCT EVALUATION

	Item	Answer	Action
6	**Competition: Are there alternative solutions that address the same problem? (Also remember question #2.)**	Yes	What is our differentiator? (Remember: Different is better than better.)
		No (Wrong answer. As a minimum the answer to question #2 is a competition.	
7	**Business Model?**		
	End product direct to end customer		
	End product through distribution/reps		
	Lease vs. buy		
	Value added channel		
	OEM		
	Channel training		
	Marketing strategy		
8	**Launch Date?**		
	Will the products still be needed?	Yes	
		No	Drop or find ways to accelerate the schedule
	What is the likelihood of additional competitors to enter the market before launch?	Low (How come?)	
		Medium	
		High	Plan mitigation
9	**Barrier of Entry**	Low	Mitigation plan
		Medium	
		High (Explain.)	
10	**Funding Needs**		
	to prototype		
	to market launch		
	to revenue (Make sure to account for the delay between early adoptors and mass market acceptance.)		

CHECKLIST FOR NEW PRODUCT EVALUATION

Item	Answer	Action
10 **Funding Needs (cont.)**		
to profit		
Return on Investment? (Section 3 vs Section 10)	Pass criteria?	Go for it
	Fail criteria?	What can be done to increase the return? To lower the investment?
11 **Scalability**		
Will it fit other markets as is? Or needs modifications?		
Production in house? Or subcontractor?		
Does the production source have the capacity to expand as needed by the business plan?	Yes?	
	No?	Strategy for future capacity expansion
12 **Extreme stress plan**		
What are the normal operating conditions?		
What are the extreme conditions to test for?		
13 **Permits required? Governments? Standards bodies? Insurance?**	Yes? List in box to the right.	
	No?	
14 **Customer support plan**	Answer must be yes. Explain the plan in the box to the right.	
15 **Warranty**		
What warranty will be offered?		
How to make sure it won't bankrupt you?		
16 **Documentation**		
What type of documentation will be required?		
What languages?		

NOTES

Chapter 1

1. "A&P History," Groceteria.com, April 6, 2009, http://www.groceteria.com/store/national-chains/ap/ap-history/.

2. Philip T. Kotler and Devin Lane Keller, introduction to *Marketing Management*, 15th ed. (London: Pearson, 2015).

3. Nat Shulman, "Energy Crisis Aided Japanese Imports," WardsAuto, May 1, 2000, http://www.wardsauto.com/news-analysis/energy-crisis-aided-japanese-imports.

4. "An Epidemic of Obesity: US Obesity Trends," Harvard T H Chan School of Public Health, accessed June 14, 2018. https://www.hsph.harvard.edu/nutritionsource/an-epidemic-of-obesity/.

5. Benjamin Siegel, "Sweet Nothing—the Triumph of Diet Soda," *American Heritage* 57, no. 3 (2006), http://www.americanheritage.com/content/sweet-nothing%E2%80%94-triumph-diet-soda-0.

6. Tala H. I. Fakhouri, Brian K. Kit, and Cynthia L. Ogden, "Consumption of Diet Drinks in the United States, 2009–2010," NCHS Data Brief, no. 109, October 2012, https://www.cdc.gov/nchs/data/databriefs/db109.pdf.

7. Mahender Singh, "New Product Forecasting," MIT OpenCourseWare (ESD 260 Lecture, September 20, 2006), https://ocw.mit.edu/courses/engineering-systems-division/esd-260j-logistics-systems-fall-2006/lecture-notes/lect5.pdf.

8. Scott D. Anthony, S. Patrick Viguerie, Evan I. Schwartz, and John Van Landeghem, "2018 Corporate Longevity Forecast: Creative Destruction Is Accelerating," Innosight, accessed June 14, 2018. https://www.innosight.com/insight/creative-destruction/.

9. Linda Rodriquez McRobbie, "Toilet Paper History: How America Convinced the World to Wipe," Mental Floss, November 7, 2009, http://mentalfloss.com/article/23210/toilet-paper-history-how-america-convinced-world-wipe.

Chapter 2

1. Bryan Mattimore, *Idea Stormers: How to Lead and Inspire Creative Breakthroughs* (San Francisco: Jossey-Bass, 2012) quoted in Lorri Freifeld, "Brainwalking: In Search of Better Brainstorms," *Training*, May 16, 2013, https://trainingmag.com/content/brainwalking-search-better-brainstorms.

2. Sylvia Ann Hewlett, Melinda Marshall, and Laura Sherbin, "How Diversity Can Drive Innovation," *Harvard Business Review*, December 2013, https://hbr.org/2013/12/how-diversity-can-drive-innovation.

3. "First Round 10 Year Project," First Round Capital, July 28, 2015, http://10years.firstround.com/.

Chapter 3

1. Akio Morita, Edwin M. Reingold, and Mitsuko Shimomura, *Made in Japan: Akio Morita and Sony* (Boston: E. P. Dutton, 1986).

2. "Historical Statistics of the United States: Colonial Times to 1970," US Census Bureau, 1975, https://archive.org/details/HistoricalStatisticsOfTheUnitedStatesColonialTimesTo1970.

3. "Investing in Innovation," Tata Group, http://www.tata.com/innovation/articlesinside/Investing-in-innovation.

4. Christopher Helman, "The Other Face of Saudi Aramco," *Forbes*, September 6, 2008, https://www.forbes.com/global/2008/0915/159.html#7d1be9dd79be.

5. "Powering Innovation," Saudi Aramco, www.saudiaramco.com/en/home/innovation/powering-innovation.html.

6. "MIT and Industry," MIT Facts, 2018, http://web.mit.edu/facts/industry.html.

7. http://samsungventures.com/

8. "Tyson Ventures," Tyson, https://www.tysonfoods.com/innovation/food-innovation/tyson-ventures.

9. "Intel Completes Acquisition of McAffee," Intel, February 28, 2011, https://newsroom.intel.com/news-releases/intel-completes-acquisition-of-mcafee/.

Chapter 4

1. Philip T. Kotler and Devin Lane Keller, *Marketing Management*, 15th ed. (London: Pearson, 2015).

2. Haim Levy and Marshall Sarnat, *Capital Investment and Financial Decisions* (Upper Saddle River, NJ: Prentice Hall, 1978) 3–73.

3. David Cravens and Nigel Piercy, *Strategic Marketing*, 8th ed. (New York City: McGraw Hill/Irwin, 2005): 34; C. Merle Crawford and C. Anthony Di Benedetto, *New Products Management*, 11th ed. (New York City: McGraw Hill Education, 2014): 52.

4. Philip A. Roussel, Kamal N. Saad, and Tamara J. Erickson, *Third Generation R&D: Managing the Link to Corporate Strategy* (Watertown, MA: Harvard Business Review Press, 1991): 1–11.

5. Joseph G. Monks, *Operations Management: Theory and Problems* (New York City: McMillan/McGraw-Hill School, 1985): 268–313.

6. Martin Kirov, "Direct Sales vs Channel Sales: Pros, Cons, and Balance," Sales Hacker, April 25, 2017, https://www.saleshacker.com/channel-sales-direct-sales-strategy/.

Chapter 5

1. John C. Chambers, Satinder K. Mullick, and Donald D. Smith, "How to Choose the Right Forecasting Techniquie," *Harvard Business Review*, July 1971, https://hbr.org/1971/07/how-to-choose-the-right-forecasting-technique.

2. Ibid.

3. Paul E. Green and Donald S. Tull, *Research for Marketing Decisions*, 4th ed. (London: Longman Higher Education, 1978).

4. Richard Feloni, "4 Lessons from the Failure of the Ford Edsel, One of Bill Gates' Favorite Case Studies," *Business Insider*, September 5, 2015, http://www.businessinsider.com/lessons-from-the-failure-of-the-ford-edsel-2015-9.

5. "Global Flavored and Functional Water Market: Growing Incidence of Obesity to Stimulate Growth, Says TMR," Transparency Market Research, June 2017, https://www.transparencymarketresearch.com/pressrelease/flavored-functional-water.htm.

6. Colin Brown, "Key Considerations in Film Finance (White Paper 3 of 4)," Slated, May 26, 2016, https://filmonomics.slated.com/key-considerations-in-film-finance-white-paper-3-of-4-67e91846d070.

7. Vijay Mahajan, Eitan Muller, and Frank M. Bass, "Diffusion of New Products: Empirical Generalizations and Managerial Uses," *Marketing Science* 14, no. 3 (1995): G79–G88, doi:10.1287/mksc.14.3.G79.

Chapter 6

1. "Disney History," D23: The Official Disney Fan Club, https://d23.com/disney-history/.

2. Wayne Pacelle, "There Is a New Normal in the Egg Industry, and It's Cage-Free," *Huffpost*, March 1, 2016, https://www.huffingtonpost.com/wayne-pacelle/there-is-a-new-normal-in_b_9359330.html.

3. Chris Brooke, "Free Range Eggs Outsell Those Laid by Caged Hens for the First Time as TV's Bake Off Inspires Baking Boom," *Daily Mail*, August 4, 2017, http://www.dailymail.co.uk/news/article-4762662/Free-range-eggs-outsell-laid-caged-hens.html.

4. W. Chan Kim and Renée Mauborgne, *Blue Ocean Strategy, Expanded Edition: How to Create Uncontested Market Space and Make the Competition Irrelevant,* (Watertown, MA: Harvard Business Review Press, 2015).

5. "About Us," Homeplate Peanut Butter, http://homeplatepb.com/about-us/.

6. David Zatz, "Creating the Plymputh, Dodge, and Chrysler Minivan: The Caravan/Voyager Development Story," Allpar.com, https://www.allpar.com/model/m/history.html.

Chapter 7

1. Mutaz M. Al-Debei, Ramzi Haddadeh, and David E. Avision, "Defining the Business Model in the New World of Digital Business," Proceedings of the Fourteenth Americas Conference on Information Systems (August 2008): 1–11, https://bura.brunel.ac.uk/bitstream/2438/2887/1/AMCIS2008.pdf.

2. http://www.constancebannister.net/

3. Chris Skinner, "Alibaba's Secret Sauce," BankNXT, November 23, 2015, https://banknxt.com/54566/alibaba-secret-sauce/.

4. Ibid.

Chapter 8

1. Louis F. Hartman and A. Leo Oppenheim, *On Beer and Brewing Techniques in Ancient Mesopotamia, Supplement to the Journal of the American Oriental Society* 10 (1950).

2. "Global Beer Market Worth USD 318.4 Billion by 2020: Analysis, Opportunities, and Forecast 2015–2020," PR Newswire, December 8, 2015, https://www.prnewswire.com/news-releases/global-beer-market-worth-usd-3184-billion-by-2020---analysis-opportunities--forecast-2015-2020-560904211.html.

3. Cortney Harraghy, Nicole Derienzo, Edlyn Ruiz, and Domenick Scherpf, "The Bud Light Brand," Anheuser-Busch, December 5, 2013, http://docplayer.net/31806622-The-bud-light-brand-december-5-th-2013-cortney-harraghy-nicole-derienzo-edlyn-ruiz-domenick-scherpf.html.

4. Philip A. Roussel, Kamal N. Saad, and Tamara J. Erickson, *Third-Generation R&D Management: Managing the Link to Corporate Strategy* (Watertown, MA: Harvard Business Review Press, 1991): 1–11; Harold Kerzner, *Project Management* 12th ed. (Hoboken, NJ: Wiley, 2017).

5. Daniel Ferry, "Boeing's Battle with Development Costs," The Motley Fool, October 26, 2012, https://www.fool.com/investing/general/2012/10/26/boeings-battle-with-development-costs.aspx.

Chapter 9

1. Geoffrey A. Moore, *Crossing the Chasm: Marketing and Selling Disruptive Products to Mainstream Customers*, 3rd ed. (New York City: HarperCollins, 2014).

Chapter 10

1. Felipe Schrieberg, "World's First Community-Owned Whisky Distillery Smashes Crowdfunding Record," *Forbes*, July 10, 2016, https://www.forbes.com/sites/felipeschrieberg/2016/07/10/worlds-first-community-owned-whisky-distillery-smashes-crowdfunding-record/#40662a868760.

2. Steve Harmon and Ann Winblad, *Zero Gravity 2.0: Launching Technology Companies in a Tougher Venture Capital World* (Bloomberg Press, 2001).

Chapter 11

1. Scott Pollack, "What, Exactly, Is Business Development?," *Forbes*, March 21, 2012, https://www.forbes.com/sites/scottpollack/2012/03/21/what-exactly-is-business-development/#fd21b497fdbb.

2. Geoffrey A. Moore, *Crossing the Chasm: Marketing and Selling Disruptive Products to Mainstream Customers*, 3rd ed. (New York City: HarperCollins, 2014).

3. Martin Zwilling, "10 Ways for Startups to Survive the Valley of Death," *Forbes*, February 18, 2013, https://www.forbes.com/sites/martinzwilling/2013/02/18/10-ways-for-startups-to-survive-the-valley-of-death/#2a04718369ef; Lisheng Wang, "Ten Tips for Avoiding the Start-up Valley of Death for Science and Technology Companies," Medium, October 19, 2016, https://medium.com/dissected-by-propel-x/ten-tips-for-avoiding-the-start-up-valley-of-death-for-science-and-technology-companies-30a7c5a6a4e2.

4. Alex Steinman, "Taco Bell Sold 100 Million Doritos Locos Tacos in 10 Weeks; Nacho Cheese Shell Taco Is Its Most Popular-Ever Item," *New York Daily News*, June 5, 2012, http://www.nydailynews.com/life-style/eats/taco-bell-sold-100-million-doritos-locos-tacos-10-weeks-nacho-cheese-shell-taco-popular-ever-item-article-1.1090326.

Chapter 12

1. Martin, "How to Launch a New Product," Cleverism, June 21, 2014, https://www.cleverism.com/how-to-launch-new-product/; David Lavenda, "10 Steps for Successfully Launching a New Product or Service," *Fast Company*, January 24, 2013, https://www.fastcompany.com/3004920/10-steps-successfully-launching-new-product-or-service.

2. Zachary Crockett, "How a Basket on Wheels Revolutionized Grocery Shopping, Priceonomics, February 18, 2016, https://priceonomics.com/how-a-basket-on-wheels-revolutionized-grocery/.

3. Paul Sloane, "A Lesson in Innovation: Why Did the Segway Fail?," InnovationManagement.se, http://www.innovationmanagement.se/2012/05/02/a-lesson-in-innovation-why-did-the-segway-fail/.

4. Jennifer Valentino-DeVries, "From Hype to Disaster: Segway's Timeline," *The Wall Street Journal*, September 27, 2010, https://blogs.wsj.com/digits/2010/09/27/from-hype-to-disaster-segways-timeline/.

5. Nir Eyal and Ryan Hoover, *Hooked: How to Build Habit-Forming Products* (London: Portfolio, 2014).

Chapter 14

1. Kevin B. Hendricks and Vinod R. Singhal, "The Effect of Product Introduction Delays on Operating Performance," *Management Science* 54, no.5 (2008): 878–892, doi:10.1287/mnsc.1070.0805; Brad Dixon, "Profits Crash When Firms Delay Product Launches," Georgia Tech News Center, February 8, 2007, http://www.news.gatech.edu/2007/02/08/profits-crash-when-firms-delay-product-launches.

2. Richard Feloni, "4 Lessons from the Failure of the Ford Edsel, One of Bill Gates' Favorite Case Studies," *Business Insider*, September 5, 2015, http://www.businessinsider.com/lessons-from-the-failure-of-the-ford-edsel-2015-9.

3. Michael Dell, "Building a Better Computer," *Success*, January 5, 2009, https://www.success.com/article/from-the-archives-michael-dell.

4. Georgia-Ann Klutke, Peter C. Kiessler, and M. A. Wortman, "A Critical Look at the Bathtub Curve," *IEE Transaction on Reliability* 52, no1 (2003), https://pdfs.semanticscholar.org/e5f4/a93868d3f206ee9dd5aed9c5f377d838f255.pdf.

Chapter 15

1. T. J. Allen, "Organizing for Product Development," WP, December 2001, https://dspace.mit.edu/bitstream/handle/1721.1/83298/PLN_0102_Allen_Org4ProdDev.pdf?sequence.

2. Nicola Clark, "The Airbus Saga: Crossed Wires and a Multibillion-Euro Delay," *The New York Times*, December 11, 2006, https://www.nytimes.com/2006/12/11/business/worldbusiness/11iht-airbus.3860198.html.

3. Vinod Khosla, "Signs It Might Be Time to Consider Hiring a CEO," TechCrunch, November 11, 2012, https://techcrunch.com/2012/11/11/signs-it-might-be-time-to-consider-hiring-a-ceo/.

4. Noam Wasserman, "The Founder's Dilemma," *Harvard Business Review*, February 2008, https://hbr.org/2008/02/the-founders-dilemma.

Chapter 16

1. Joseph G. Monks, *Operations Management: Theory and Problems* (New York City: McMillan/McGraw-Hill School, 1985): 591–622.

2. "System/360 Announcement," IBM, April 7, 1964, https://www-03.ibm.com/ibm/history/exhibits/mainframe/mainframe_PR360.html.

3. Larry Dwyer, "Douglas DC-3," The Aviation History Online Museum, Updated November 24, 2014, http://www.aviation-history.com/douglas/dc3.html.

Chapter 17

1. "Kingdom Death: Monster 1.5," Kickstarter, https://www.kickstarter.com/projects/poots/kingdom-death-monster-15; TechRaptor, "Kingdom Death Lore Interview with Adam Poots Gen Con 2017," YouTube, September 13, 2017, https://www.youtube.com/watch?v=uGrs5x-5RJE.

Chapter 18

1. "FDA Approves Viagra," History, March 27, 1998, https://www.history.com/this-day-in-history/fda-approves-viagra.

2. "Tyson Foods, Inc.," Company-Histories.com, http://www.company-histories.com/Tyson-Foods-Inc-Company-History.html.

Chapter 19

1. Vikrant Khanna, "9 Emotional Product Buying Motives of Customers," Preserve Articles, http://www.preservearticles.com/201103154543/9-emotional-product-buying-motives-of-customers.html.

2. Nir Eyal and Ryan Hoover, *Hooked: How to Build Habit-Forming Products* (London: Portfolio, 2014).

3. Carita Porthan, "Nokio Colour and Material Design Strategy," IDSA, 2013, http://www.idsa.org/awards/idea/design-strategy/nokia-colour-and-material-design-strategy.

4. W. Chan Kim and Renée Mauborgne, *Blue Ocean Strategy, Expanded Edition: How to Create Uncontested Market Space and Make the Competition Irrelevant*, (Watertown, MA: Harvard Business Review Press, 2015).

5. Dan Good, "The Pet Rock Captured a Moment and Made Its Creator a Millionaire," ABC News, April 1, 2015, https://abcnews.go.com/US/pet-rock-captured-moment-made-creator-millionaire/story?id=30041318.

6. Geoffrey James, "The 7 'Emotional Hooks' for B2B Selling," MoneyWatch, Updated August 3, 2009, https://www.cbsnews.com/news/the-7-emotional-hooks-for-b2b-selling/.

Chapter 20

1. Peter Loftus, "Merck Wins Victory vs Gilead in Hep C Drug Dispute," MarketWatch, March 22, 2016, https://www.marketwatch.com/story/merck-wins-victory-vs-gilead-in-hep-c-drug-dispute-2016-03-22.

2. Matthew Belloni, "Warner Bros. Settles 'Hangover II' Tattoo Lawsuit (Exclusive)," *The Hollywood Reporter*, June 20, 2011, https://www.hollywoodreporter.com/thr-esq/warner-bros-settles-hangover-ii-203377.

Chapter 21

1. Jean-Philippe Deschamps, "Governing Innovation in Practice: The Role of the Board of Directors," InnovationManagement.se, 2013, http://www.innovationmanagement.se/2013/05/21/governing-innovation-in-practice-the-role-of-the-board-of-directors/.

2. Michael Useem, Dennis Carey, and Ram Charan, "How Boards Can Innovate," *Harvard Business Review*, May 21, 2014, https://hbr.org/2014/05/how-boards-can-innovate.

Chapter 22

1. Benjamin Weyers, "Global Expansion of US Fast Food Restaurants: A Case Study of McDonald's in Italy," University of Connecticut, May 6, 2012, https://opencommons.uconn.edu/cgi/viewcontent.cgi?referer=https://www.google.com/&httpsredir=1&article=1223&context=srhonors_theses.

2. Thomas B. McVey, "International Business Planning Checklist," 2009, http://www.williamsmullen.com/sites/default/files/wm-url-files/02-International-Planning-Checklist.pdf.

Conclusion

1. Max Tegmark, *Life 3.0: Being Human in the Age of Artificial Intelligence* (New York City: Knopf, 2017).

2. Aidan Connolly, "How Digital Technology is Disrupting Chicken & Eggs," Alltech, http://ag.alltech.com/en/blog/flocking-digital-future-poultry-technology.

INDEX

ABOUT THE AUTHOR

Arie Brish spent more than thirty years contributing to global innovations in diverse industries in a variety of executive roles, including general manager and CEO, as well as board of director and advisory roles. He has participated in different aspects of the development of hundreds of new products, learning from successes and mistakes. As he puts it, "I get bored quickly, and during the twenty years I worked for Motorola they were kind enough to let me move around the company every few years to serve multiple business units, with different applications, various technologies, and an eclectic customer base all over the world. I am very grateful for those opportunities."

Brish started his career in 1978 as an R&D engineer for National Semiconductors, designing the first 32-bit microprocessors in the industry. The product was superior relative to other competitors at the time. Eventually, however, he says, "Intel and

Motorola surpassed us because they did a better job in all the other disciplines that must support a new product success, such as manufacturing, marketing, sales, quality control, to name a few. This is exactly the motto of this book: It takes more than a good idea to make a commercially successful product."

Mr. Brish currently serves his global clients as a groundbreaker in growth strategies, commercialization of new paradigms, change leadership, and turnaround.

Made in the
USA
Middletown, DE

77370816R00224